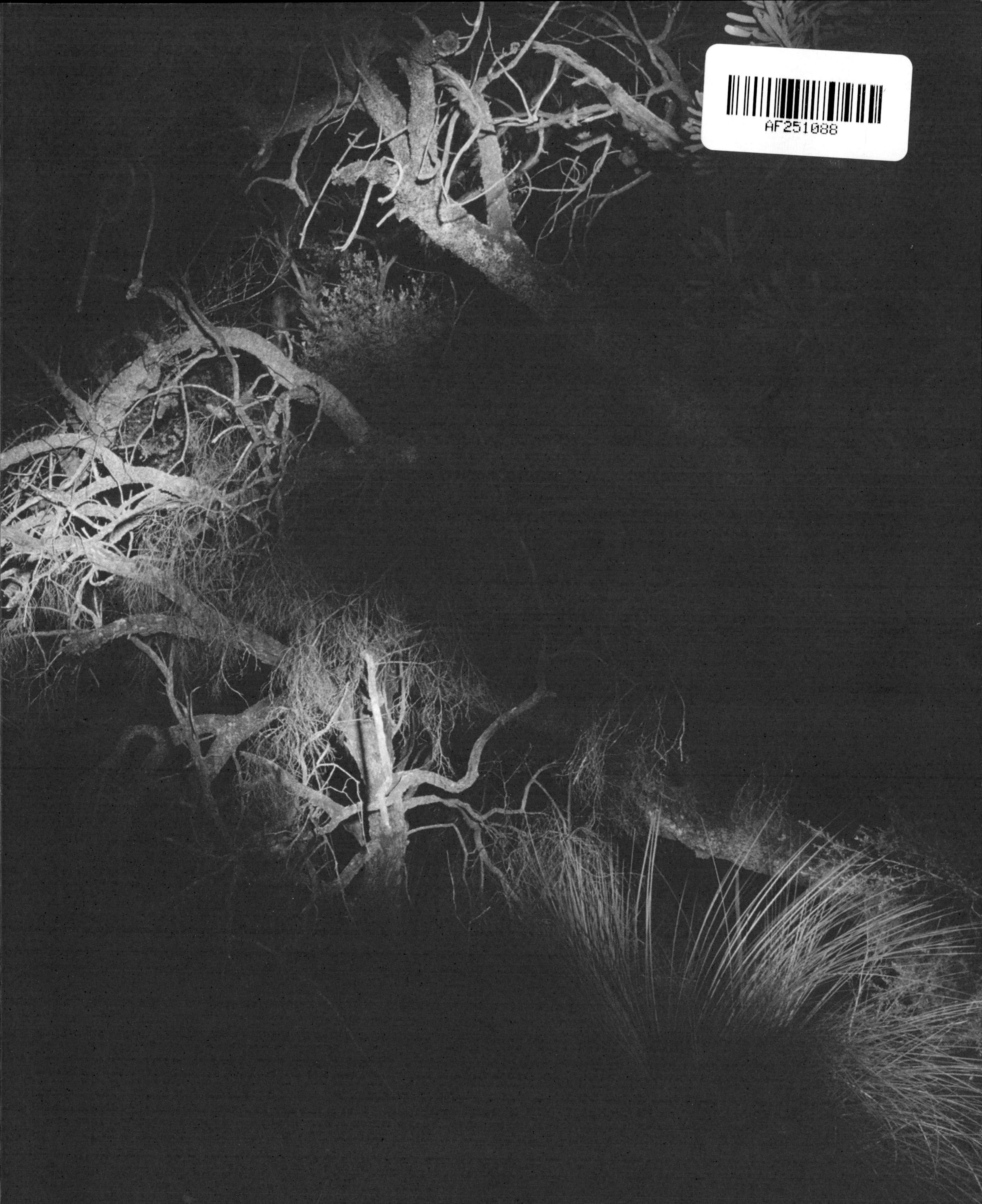
AF251088

Marian Drew
photographs + video works

foreword by Geoffrey Batchen

essays by
Dr Caroline Jordan
Anne Kirker
Dr Brigitta Olubas
Russell Storer
Marian Drew

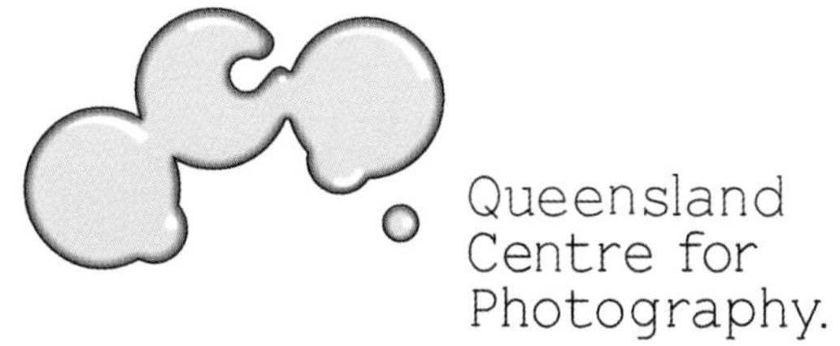

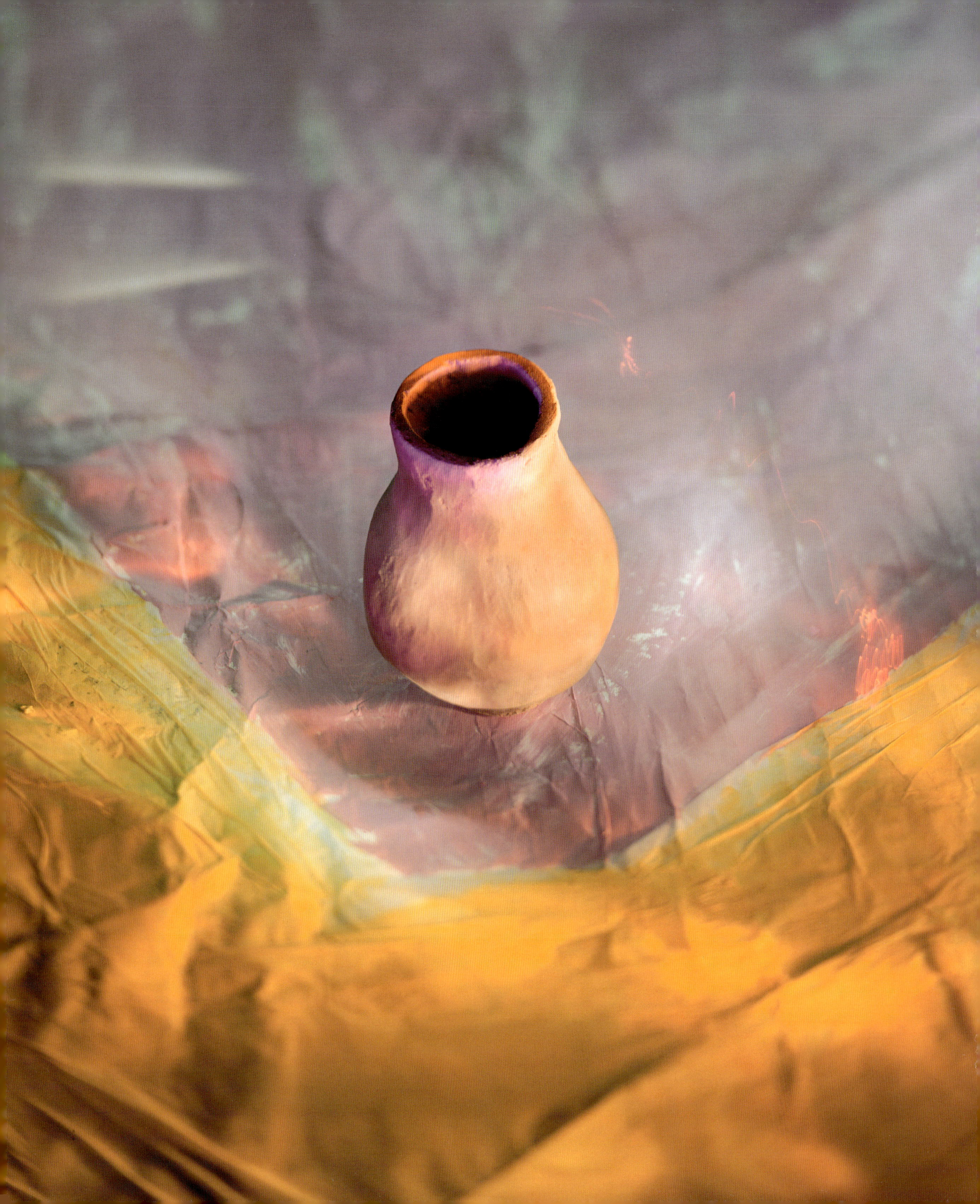

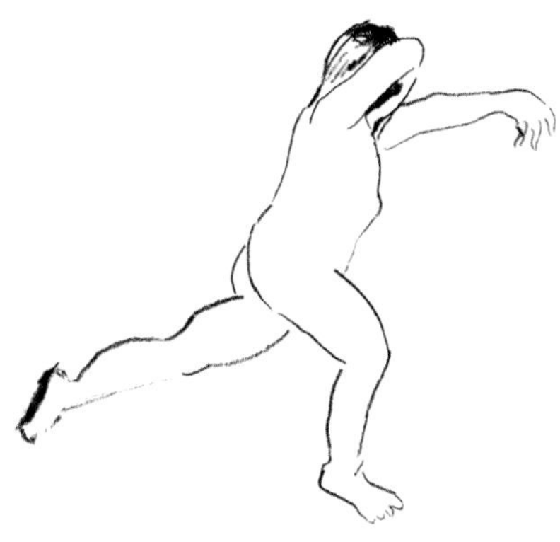

opposite: *Pink Strawberry Honey* (1992)

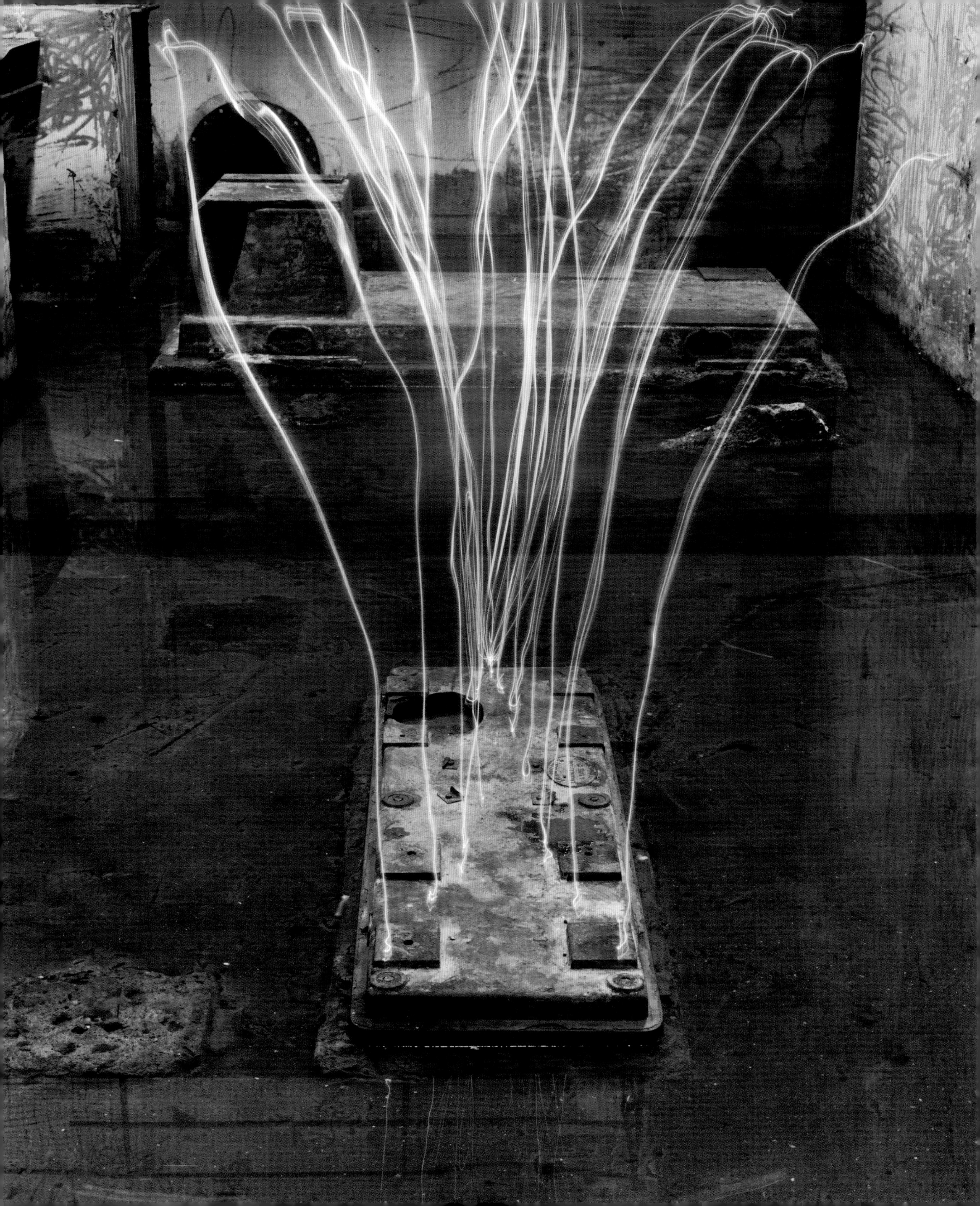

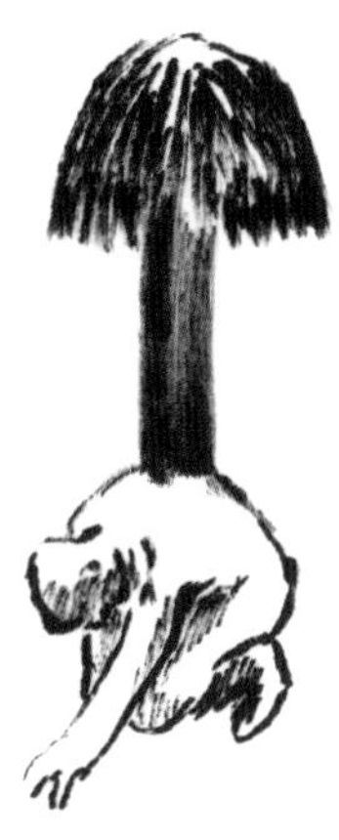

The Evidential Force of Marian Drew

The important thing about photography, according to Roland Barthes, is "that the photograph possesses an evidential force, and that its testimony bears not on the object but on time." The work of Marian Drew constitutes a creative, often playful dialogue with this proposition, offering us pictures of various objects permeated by time, or perhaps they are actually pictures of temporality itself, transformed into a visible object and thereby extended and multiplied, accumulated and transposed, smeared across the picture plane or captured in a hardened instant of photographic illusion. That her images are often manipulated, either before the camera or in the darkroom (or both) merely places this work all the more firmly within the history of photography. For such manipulations have been central to photography from the beginning, found as much in the work of Talbot, Daguerre and Bayard as in that of Man Ray, Avedon, or Gursky. As a form of representation devoted to being rather than resemblance, testifying to something's irrefutable place in space/time but not to that thing's truthful appearance, photography's apparent realism has always been deceptive. Drew's heightened colour, theatrical compositions and layered imagery signal that her work is indeed *worked*, displacing any lingering misconceptions that photography involves mere reflection. The world she reveals to us is one that has been overtly created rather than simply taken. And yet, and yet - it has to be said that the evidential force of these pictures is still generated by our lingering faith (a theological, and not entirely rational, investment on our part) in photography's privileged relationship to the real. The fact that these are *photographs* matters, even when it shouldn't. This is where the play comes in. Marian Drew has made a career out of exploring the real unreality of the photograph, testing the limits of both our faith and her chosen medium. This survey exhibition outlines her exploration in full, compressing her own artistic chronology into a single visual experience, and allowing us to witness her testimony in all of its perversely wondrous permutations.

Geoffrey Batchen

Professor
Art History
Graduate Center, University of New York

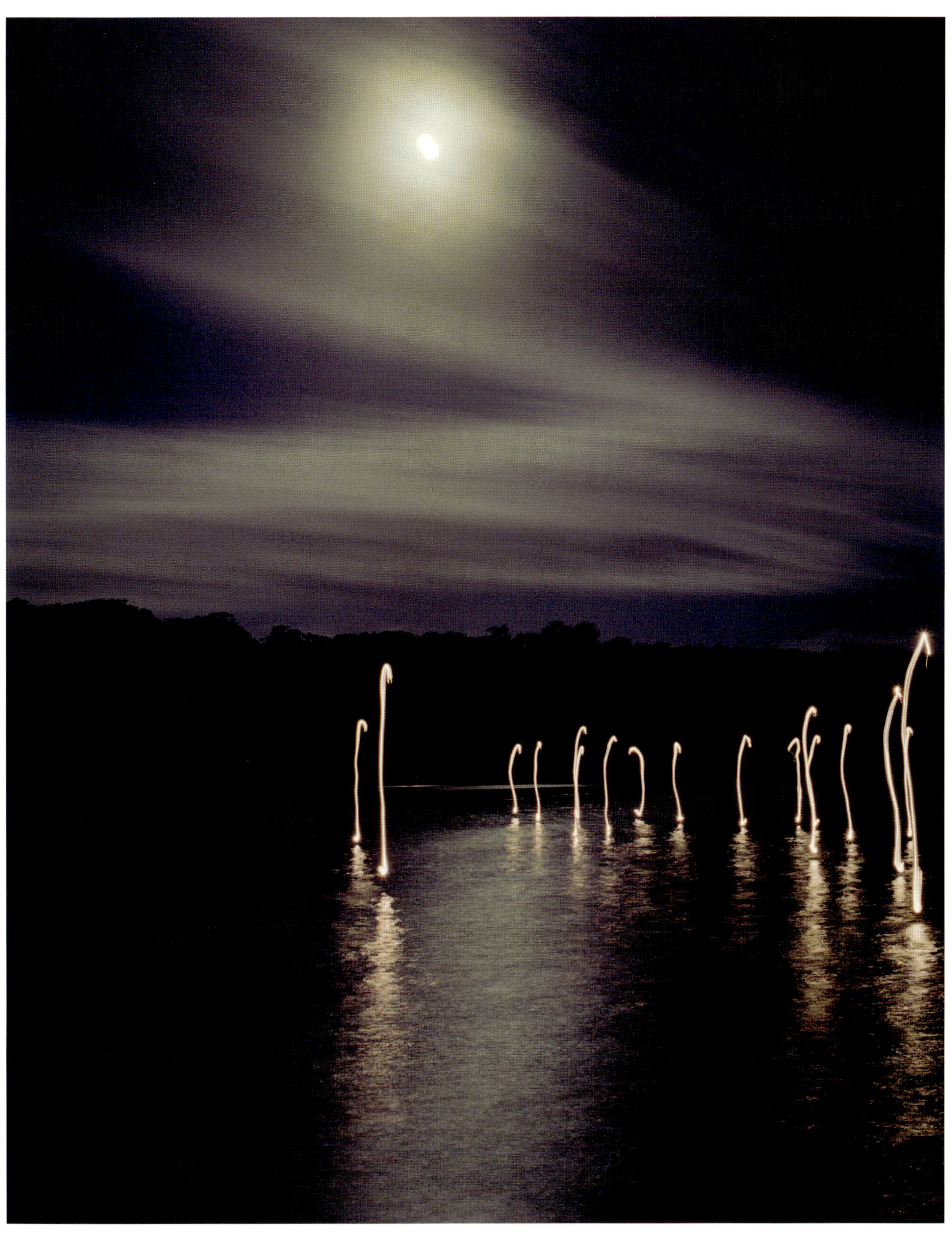

Light sticks Lake McKenzie (2006)

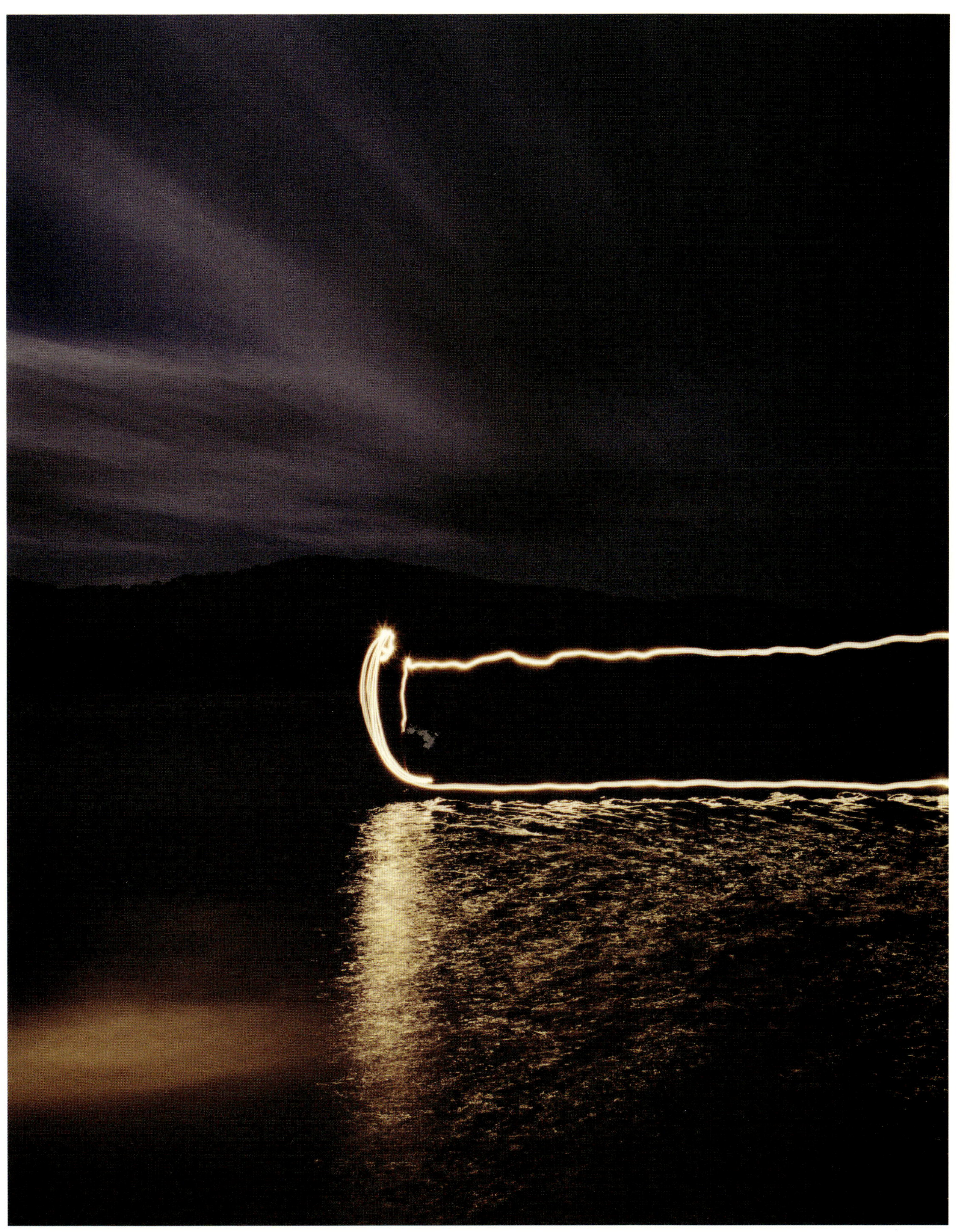

Boat Lake McKenzie (2006)

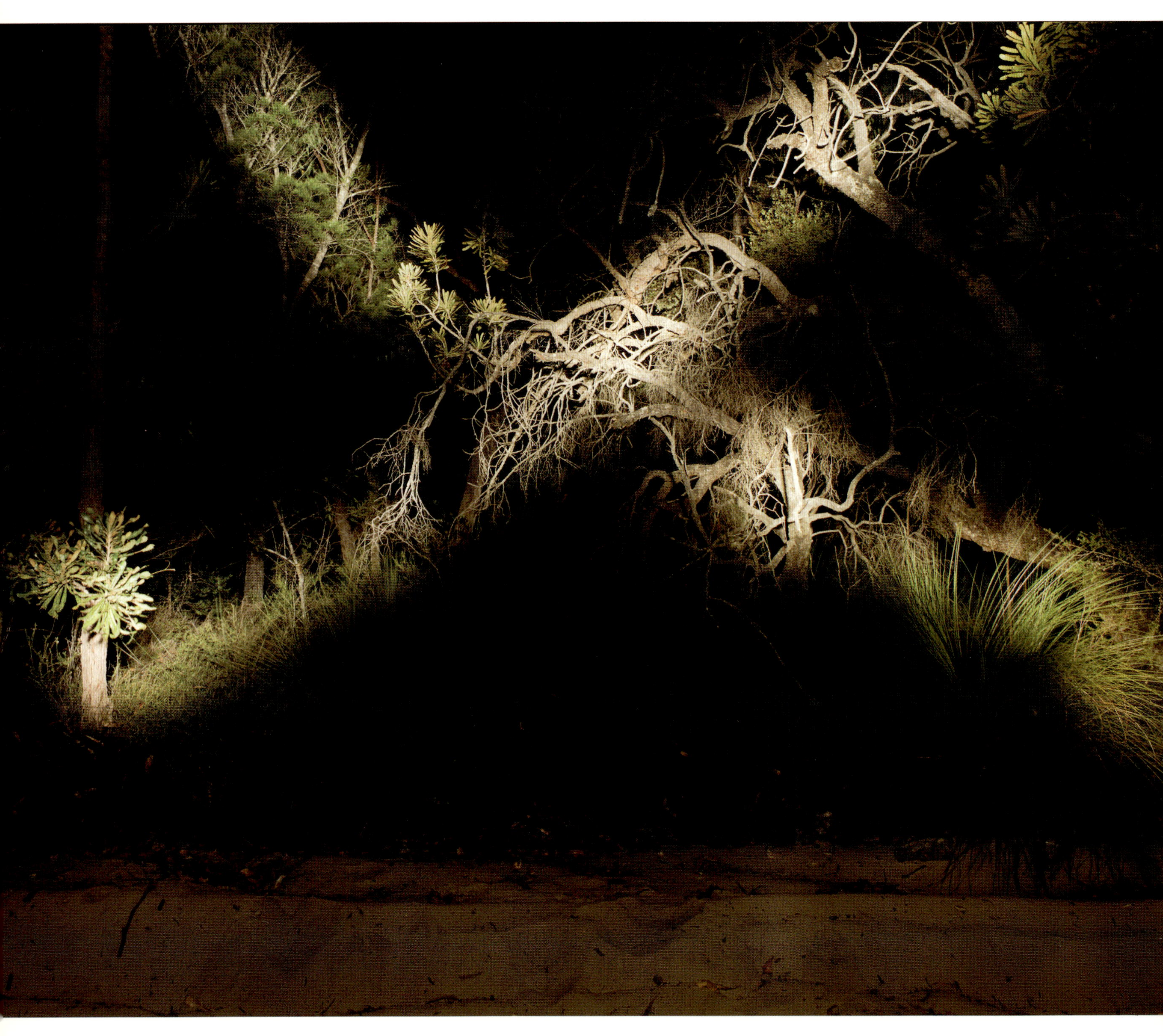

 Fraser Cross (2006)

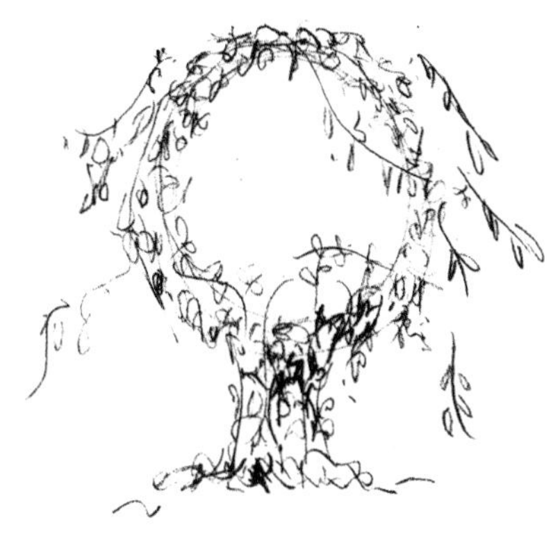

Feeling your way: inside the landscape

I have a distrust of photographing with the camera... it freezes things from a particular viewpoint and puts the viewer outside of the scene. It imposes a western philosophy onto this idea of landscape which I'm sure has got nothing to do with remembering Aboriginal history or creating our sense of place from living here now. I think photographs are actually quite destructive in helping us understand who we are and how we fit in to the world.[1]

Marian Drew is a photographer who is profoundly sceptical about the ability of her primary tool, the camera, to reveal any kind of truth. The things that the modern camera is designed to do well when pointed at the landscape -- capturing the fleeting moment or creating an artfully composed picturesque view — she sees as misleading and potentially dangerous. Looking at the landscape through the lens of the camera, it is all too easy to succumb to the machine's technical flattery and fail to understand, let alone transcend, its control over our vision. Worse, it encourages us to maintain our distance; we split the eye and the body, the viewer and the subject. For Drew, breaking down this separation and abdicating the sense of omniscience conferred by the camera is mandatory. Instead she looks for provisional ways around the camera's shortcomings, feeling her way, deliberately trying not to know where she might end up. The journey, the process, the experience, becomes as, if not more, important than the end result.

Resolving the problems presented by working with (or against) the camera in the landscape has been important in the evolution of Drew's performative method and vocabulary of signs. Drew has never been interested so much in documenting the landscape as in intervening in it, working on it from the inside, leaving ephemeral marks or traces on it. She sees the landscape itself as profoundly cultural, steeped in desire, memory and history. Accordingly, she has used it as a vehicle to work through pressing issues of belonging, place and identity. Progressively, investigations of personal myth and subjective experience have merged with broader concerns: the dawning of the cost of the loss of Indigenous civilisation in her part of the country, the impact of whitefella ways on the environment.

Drew's barefoot country childhood amid the natural abundance of tropical Queensland has crucially shaped

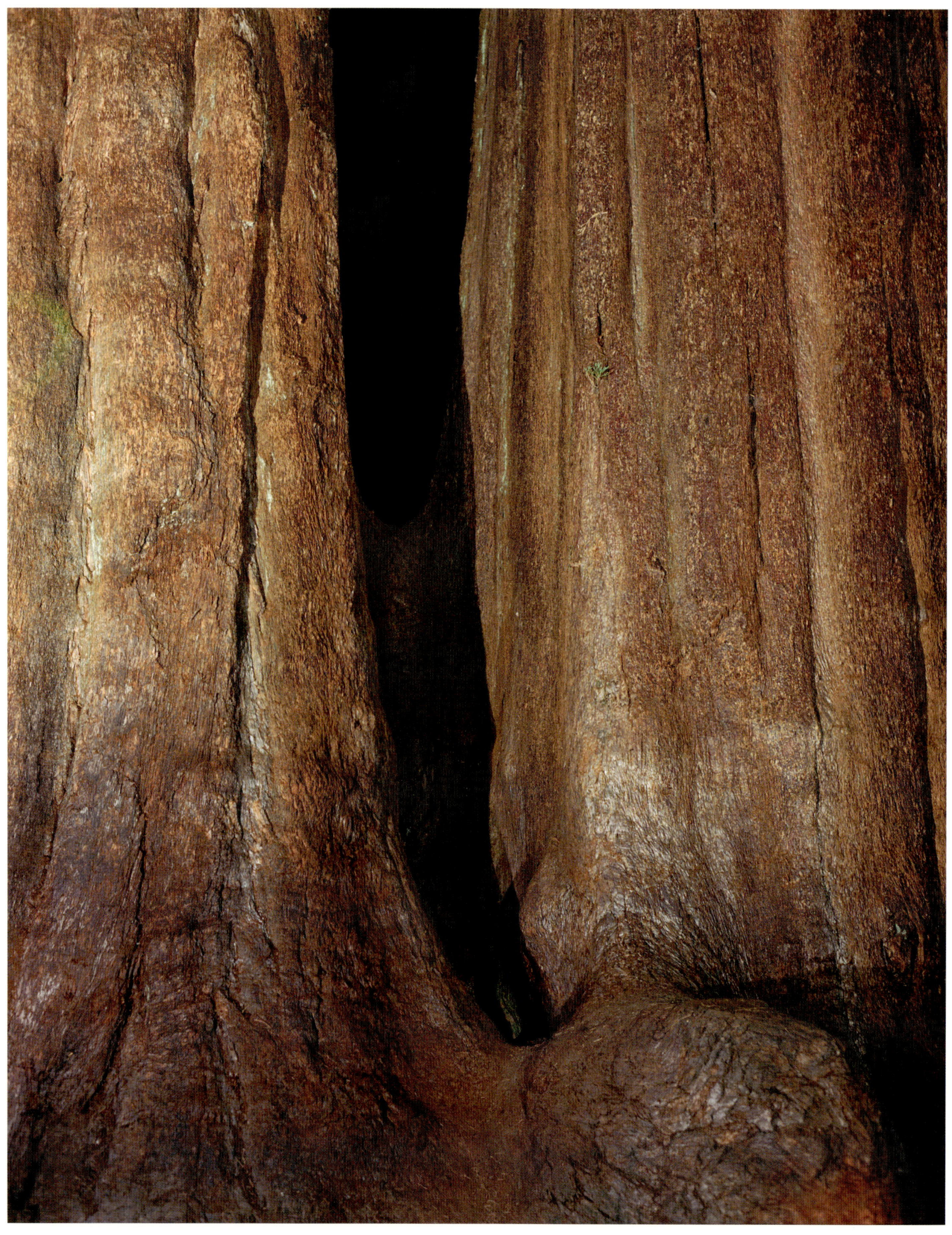

12   *Sequoia* (1995)

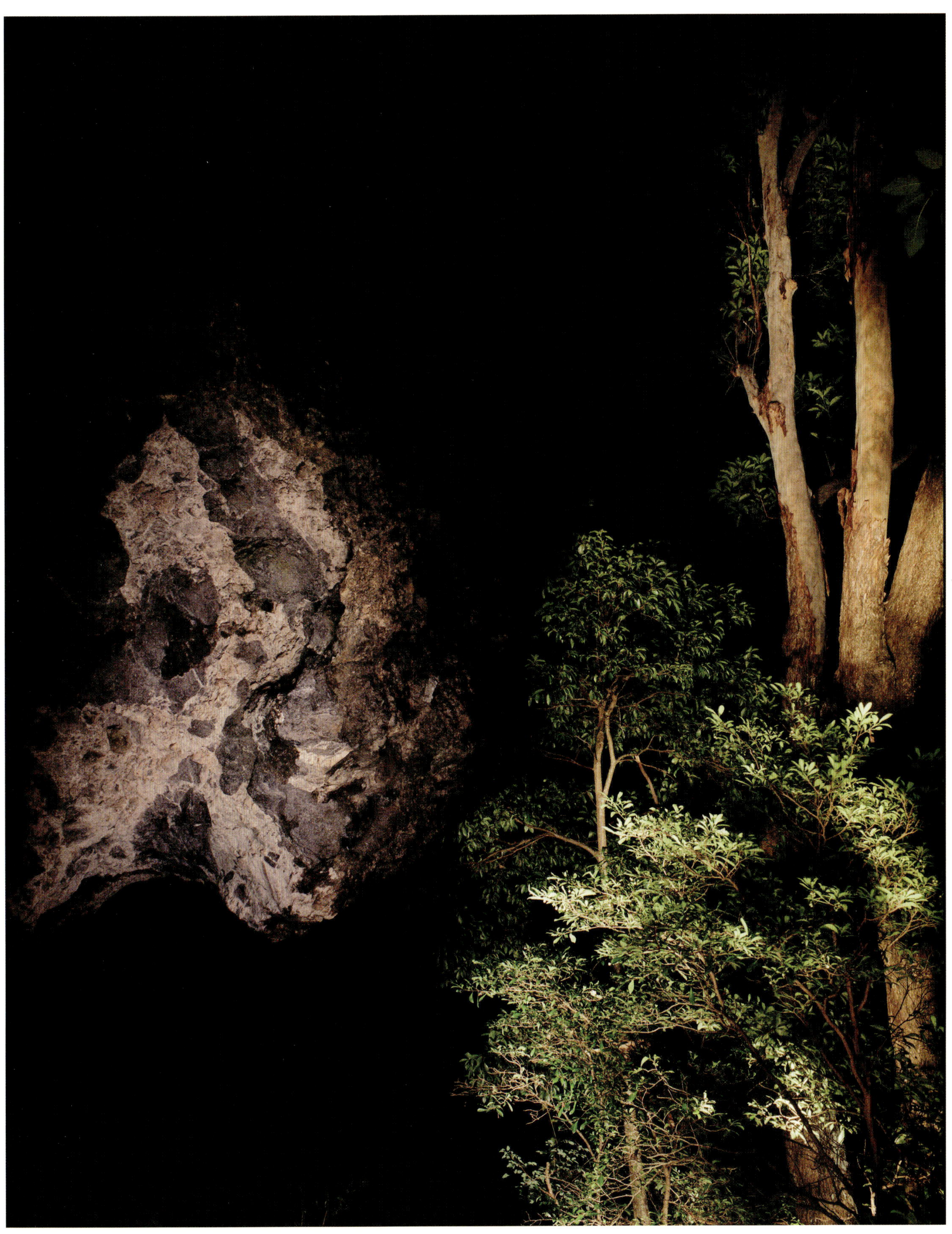

Chinese Landscape Gold Coast (2006)

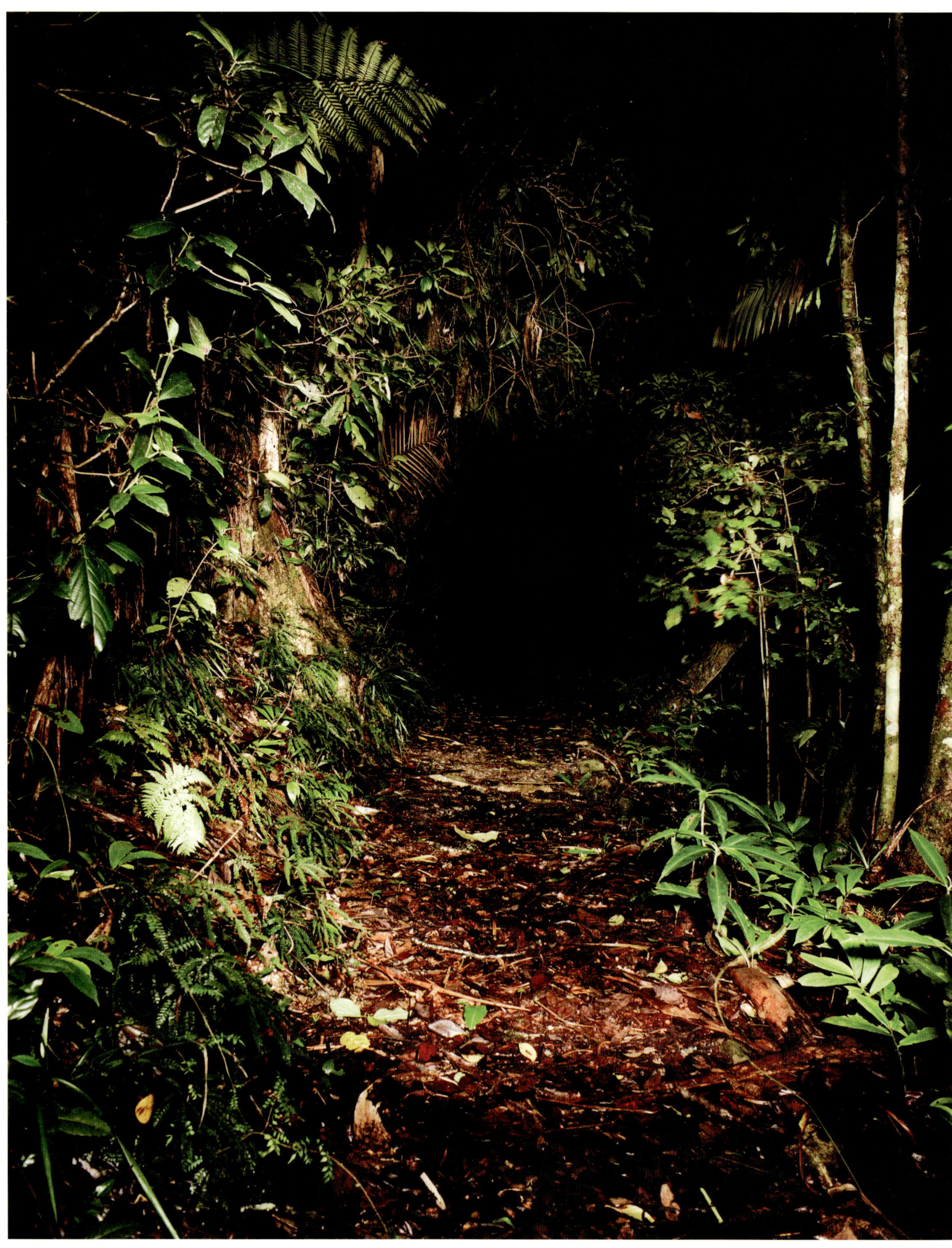

   Inlet Mackay Highlands (2006)

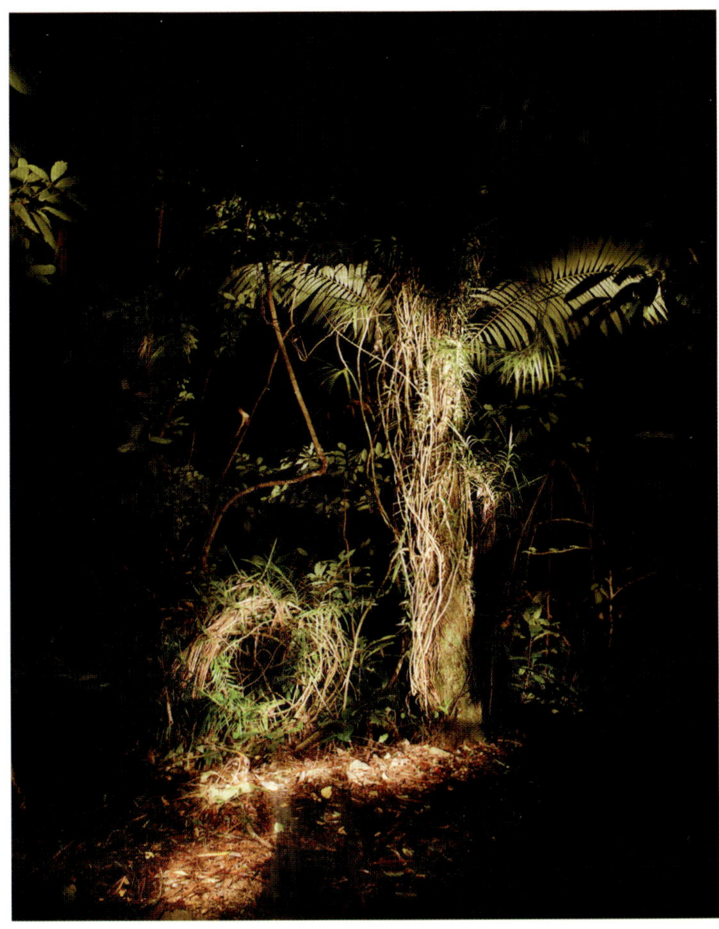

Tree + circle Whitsunday (2006)

Untitled (2000)

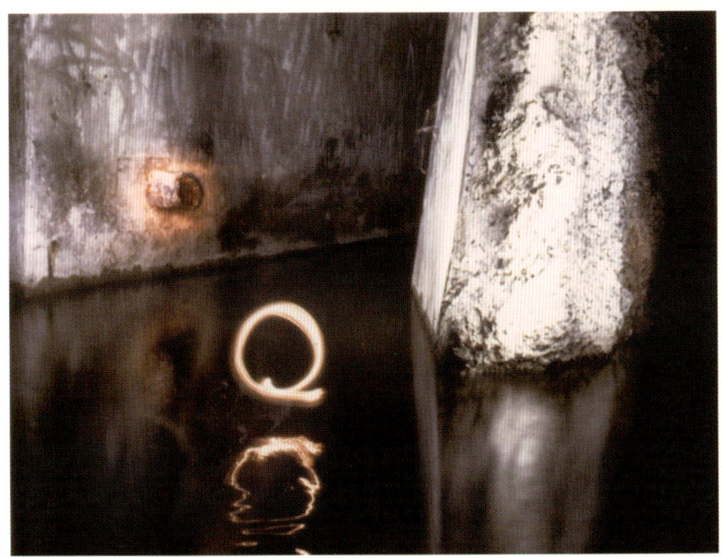

her connection to the bush, which remains a touchstone and her most vivid imaginative resource. The experience of leaving the country for periods of work in Germany and the US has also been important in this respect. Travel has intensified her attachment to the Australian landscape, and at the same time has prompted her to probe the relationship more critically. Two series of works have been conceived directly on return from these periods overseas, one looking at the place of native animals in our lives (the *Still Life* series) and one at the Indigenous haunting of her locality (the *Wynnum History* series). Unsurprisingly, given her record of experimentation with landscape, Drew has also received commissions from public bodies to explore landscape sites (the *Powerhouse* and *National Parks* series).

Drew was commissioned to record the Brisbane Powerhouse in 1999, prior to its obliteration as an industrial site and re-invention as a Performing Arts Complex. At the time the abandoned building consisted of a series of dark, partially-flooded chambers, studded with the monumental shells of dead machinery. Although entering this eerie and possibly poisonous space was an intimidating prospect, Drew literally waded into it:

I had to walk in there with my knee-high boots, making sure there weren't any holes under the murky water. I would open the camera up and walk in with my torch and do this little action in front of the camera...I like to get behind things and move all around things...so it seems to come out of the space itself rather than being imposed on it.

Drew's strategy, after sketching ideas and making several reconnaissance trips, was to go into the space alone and try to express it organically by registering her movements around it. To do this she "opened the camera up", that is, left the shutter open to register changes in the image over time. The torch she carried was used to make gestural marks in front of the camera, making manifest her presence and intervention in the watery landscape. For the artist, going into the broken, polluted site and making marks there were symbolic actions. They were a type of exorcism aimed at recolonising and rehabilitating an environment that had become uninhabitable: *I wanted to use the light and the drawing as a way of gently claiming back the space for human habitation... it's a leaving of a kind of gentle stroke of activity that shifts the function of the spot to something else.* The resulting images remake the brooding Powerhouse interiors as a flickering canvas, scribbled over with expressive marks, and redefined by elemental shapes – the circle, the rectangle – drawn with light.

More recently, in 2005/2006, Drew was commissioned by the Environmental Protection Agency to photograph heritage national parks in tropical North Queensland. As in the Powerhouse series, Drew's aim was to import a human idea into the environment by entering into it and leaving her mark. This time, however, the purpose was not to reclaim an unnatural environment as fit for humans, but to show the natural forest as something already imagined and brought into being by humans, as within rather than outside of culture. While Drew's marks within the rainforest indicate a landscape remade though human presence, there are no visible figures. The marks themselves are either scrawls or simple abstract shapes. In the forest, she was wary of being too literal, or falling into the sentimental or pictorial clichés associated with the sublime landscape: *It's quite a struggle finding marks that you can make in the forest that are appropriate. I didn't want to be too pictorial. It becomes very, very reduced in terms of crosses and circles.*

Drew says the problem of how to photograph the rainforest has preoccupied her since 1981:

In the very first images when I would go back home [to Bundaberg] from Canberra, the only thing I could do was collage bits and pieces. I was trying to recreate this sense of being so surrounded, embraced, but you can never photograph like that with a single lens image. It came back to that original challenge –how do I represent these ideas we have about the forest, with a camera?

For Drew, the challenge of photographing the rainforest is twofold: it is (over)loaded with metaphor and it is an all-embracing sensory experience impossible to represent in two dimensions. Because she rejects the camera's monocular, detached view as inadequate and suspect, she looked for routes into the site that would bring the body and its senses more into play. Working at night was important in shifting her perceptual position to that of an explorer encountering the landscape for the first time, or to that of a child:

It was that childlike discovery and memory and idea of mystery that children have and love to create in those

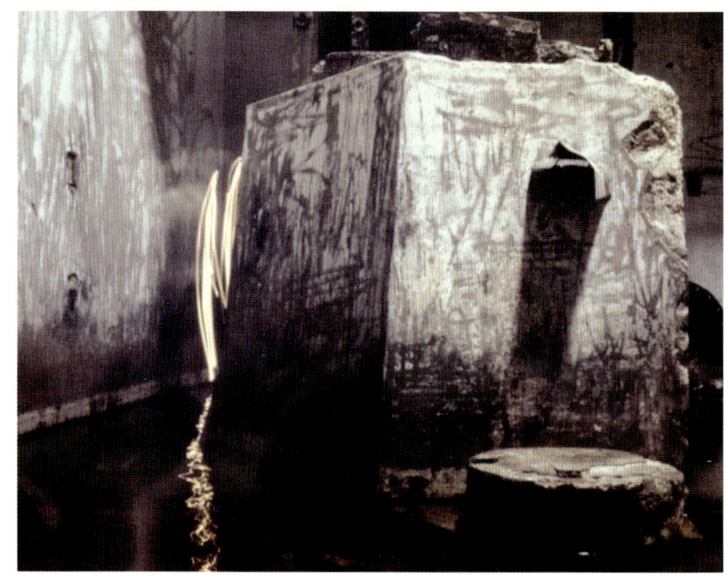

Monolith (2000)

Cross and figure (2000)

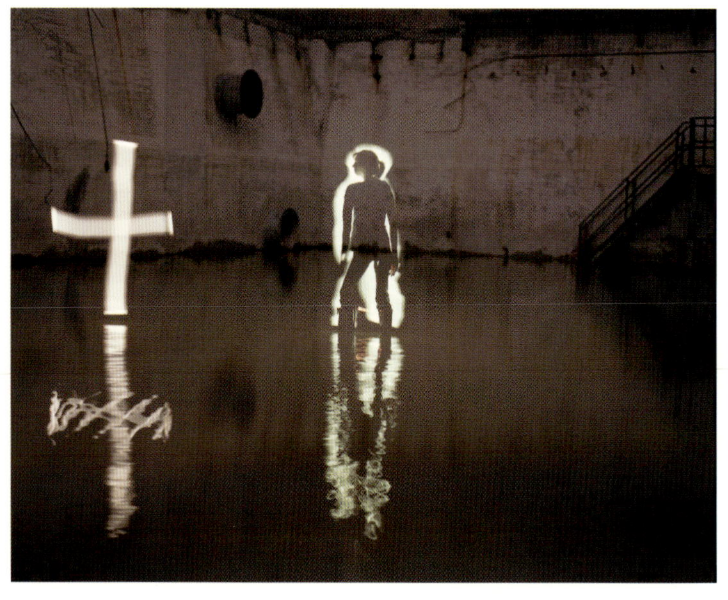

  opposite: *Blue rectangle* (2000)

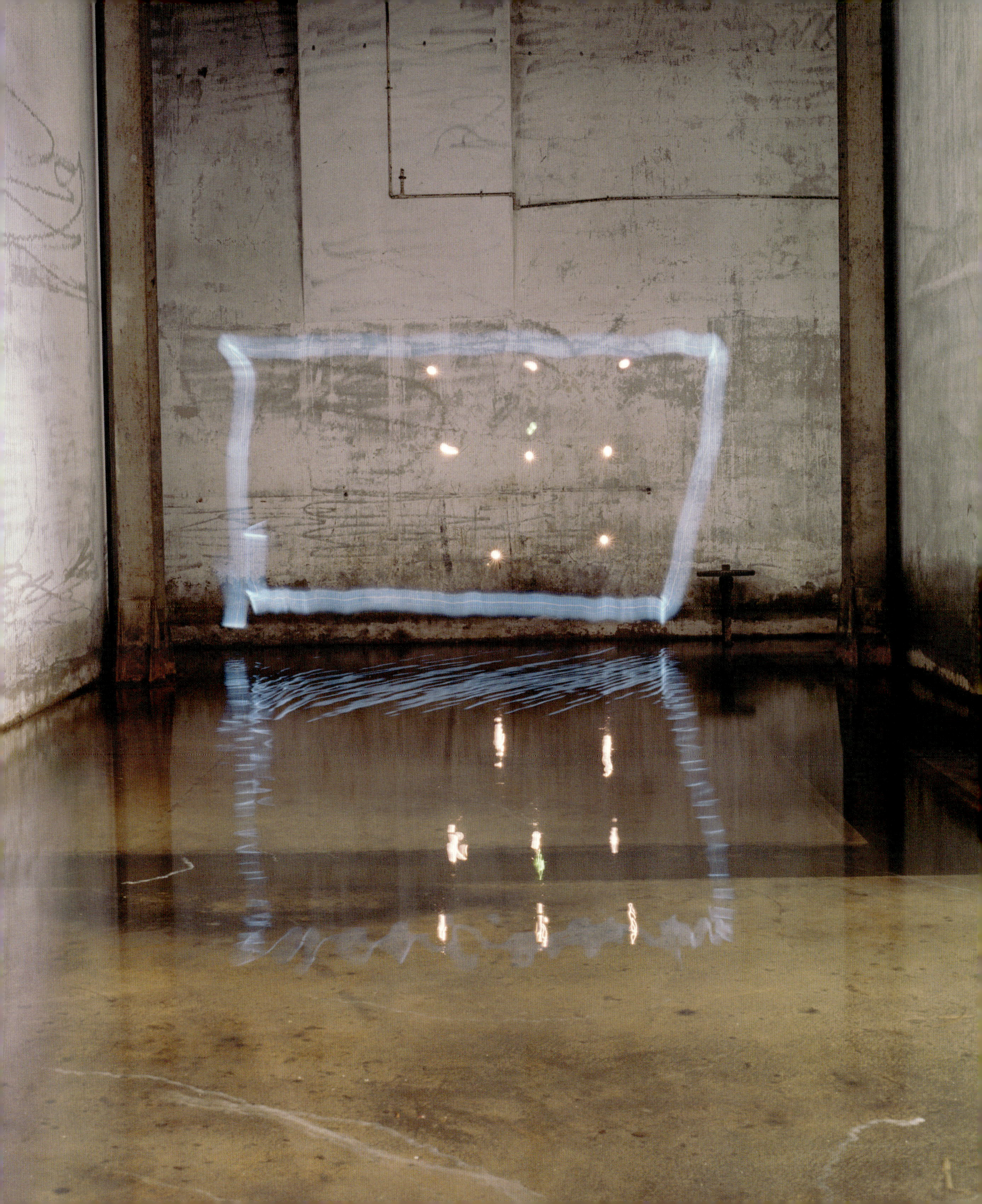

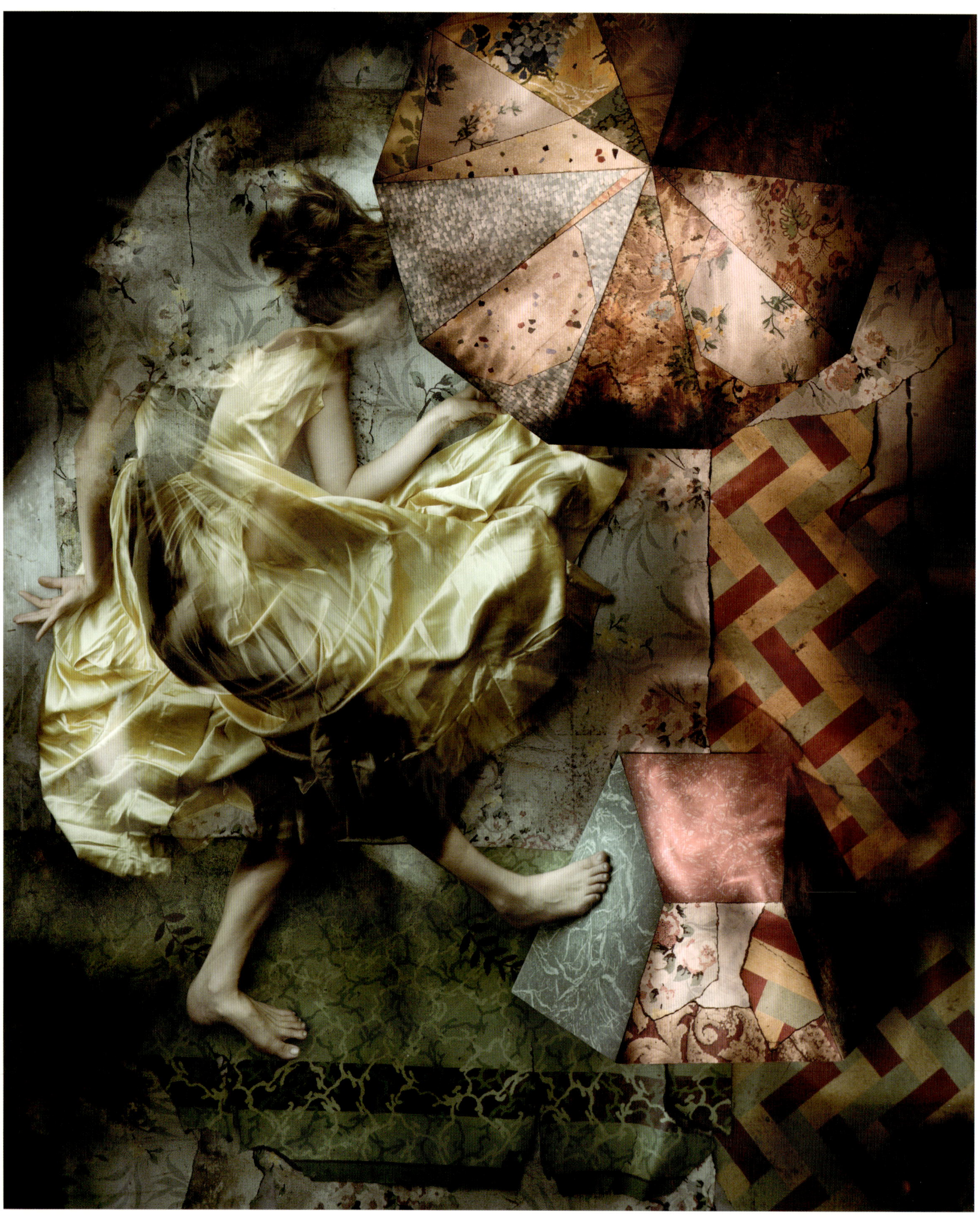

18   *Satin and lino* (1992)

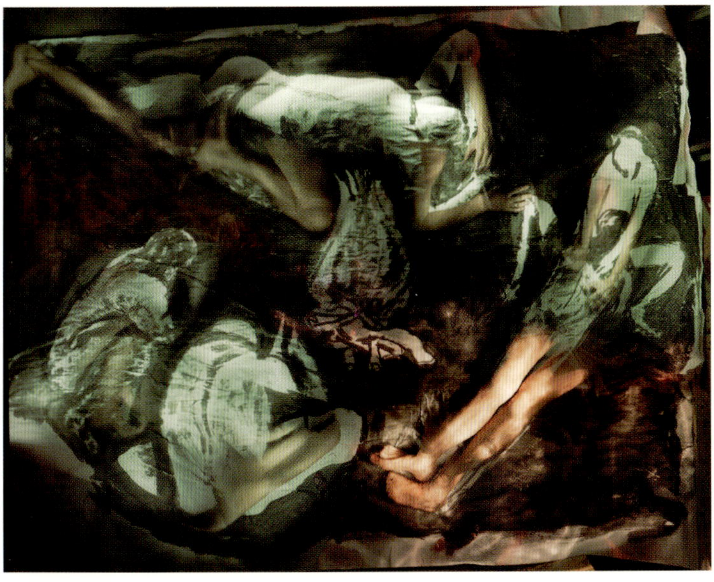

Skinning (1992)

Bogman (1992)

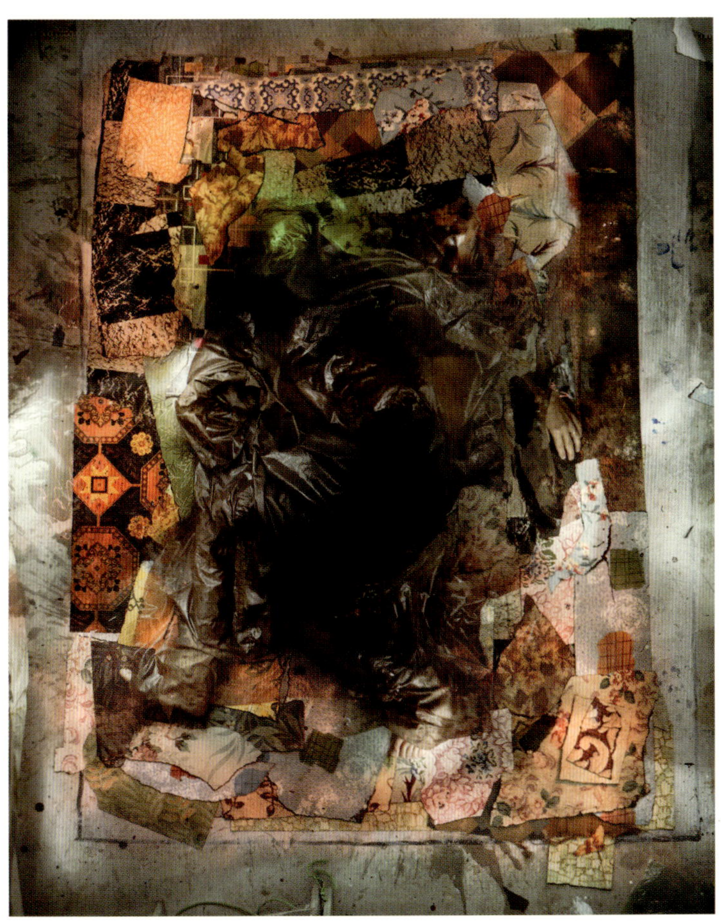

Drew's nocturnal encounters with the forest enabled her to feel her way into it, to invoke a sense of mystery, and to play with the possibilities of hand-held light. Some reflect traces of frenetic activity left behind by the waving of her torch around objects, while others gently evoke "sacred sites" in the landscape through glowing illumination. Sometimes Drew's lighting monumentalises giant trees, while in others it seems to poke fun at them. The trees in *Tree + Circle Mackay* are quirky sticks and balls, as if drawn by a child. *Inlet Mackay Highlands* boils down the dense tangle of vegetation into a spooky primal hole, evoking both the sense of awe and the sense of humour inherent in the child's-eye view of the forest.

Drew's bodily, experiential method of entering into the arena of these landscapes has developed out of earlier studio work in which the body imaged in performance is a key element. In the *Wynnum History* series of 1990 to 1992, the body is the means to explore feelings of unhomeliness in the landscape and the gradual process of recovering identity through the exploration of buried memory. Of all Drew's works, this series deals most directly with the issue of the Indigenous occupation of the landscape. This was to the fore of public consciousness in the early 1990's, culminating in the Mabo and Wik landrights decisions of 1992 and 1996 respectively. Rather than proceeding programmatically as a response to contemporary political debate, however, the series was sparked by the artist's feelings of confused identity on her return from a stint in an overseas studio:

The Wynnum History works were made coming back from New York so there was a context of New York and back into Brisbane. There was this idea of knowing who you are as drawn from your history and your environment. That question was quite pressing coming back from New York. I didn't really know who I was, I didn't know my history and I didn't know my environment.

Drew's process of coming to terms with this crisis of identity was to research the history of colonial contact with Indigenous people around Brisbane; in places like the former penal colony of St Helena Island in Moreton Bay and the bayside suburb of Wynnum where she lived. Drew's readings in local Indigenous history led her

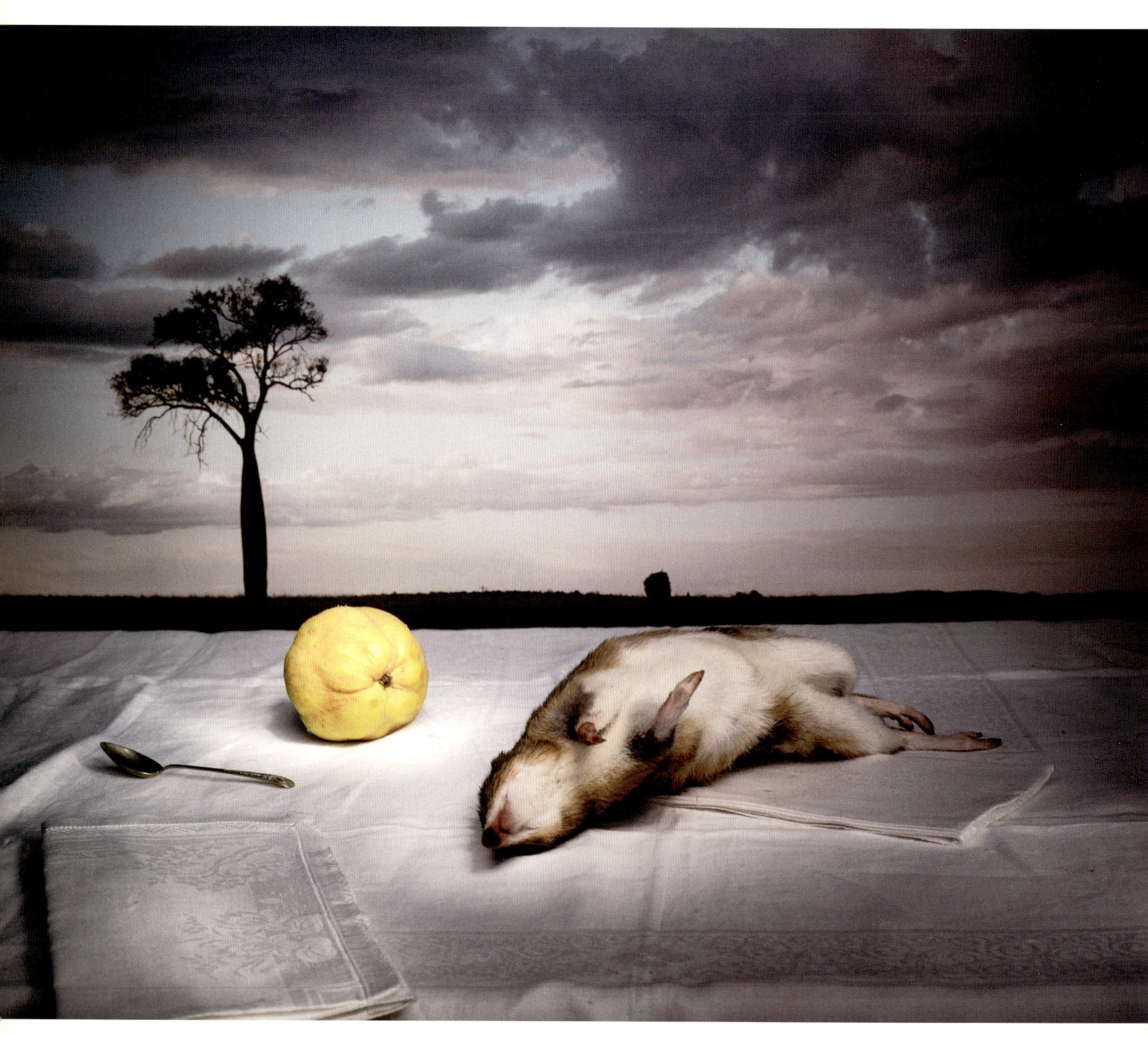

  Bandicoot with Quince (2005)

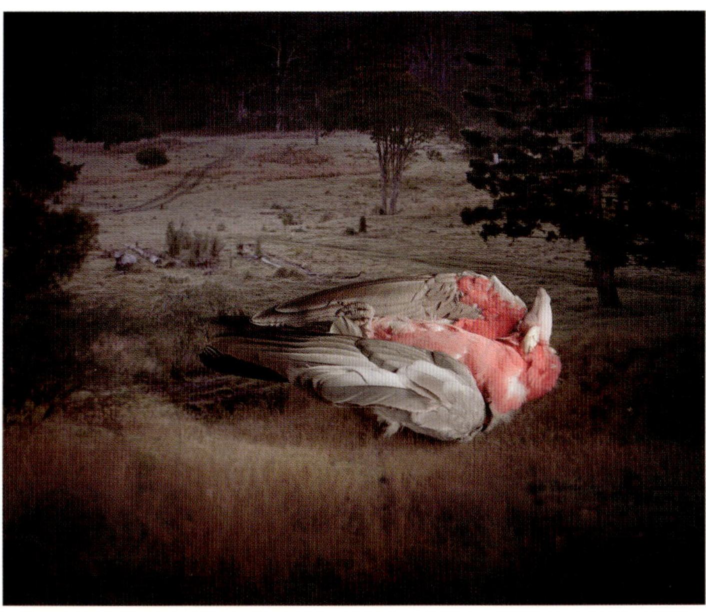

Galah in landscape (2003)

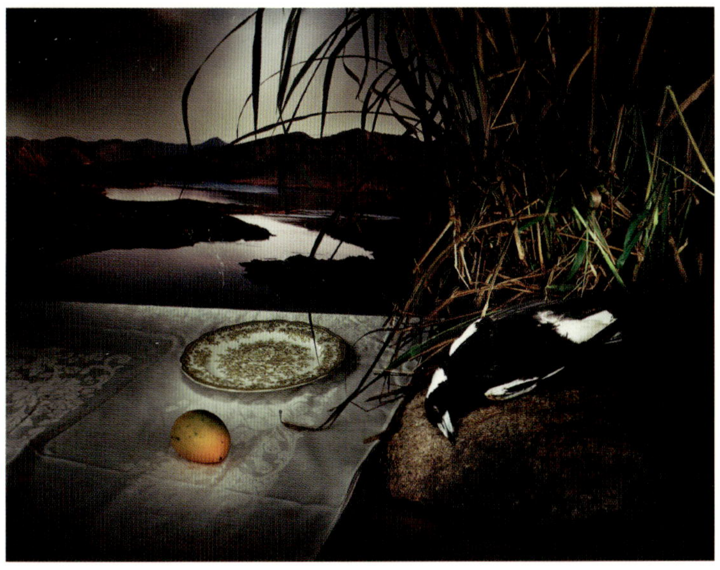

Magpie with Pawpaw (2005)

to explore sites such as old corroborree grounds in the Redlands area around Wynnum, as described by J. G. Steele in *Aboriginal Pathways in South East Queensland and the Richmond River.*[2] She found these had all been completely obliterated, many as recently as the 1970's: *I went to those places and there was an old people's home on top of one or a farm so they didn't exist anymore. The only thing that exists is the records and memories of how things were.* With the affect of the sites themselves drained away, Drew was not drawn to photographing them. Instead, she distilled the sites and their memories into a metaphor of archaeology; they became *images about how things sink into the ground, how the past melts or is retained somehow in the floors on which we walk.* At the time, Drew's husband, artist Bruce Reynolds, was employed on his own suburban archaeological excavations, in a series of works that used the layers of linoleum laid down and left like substrata on the floors of derelict houses. Drew used these works to stage photographs such as *Wet Figure on Lino*, in which her own body, curled in a foetal position and seen from above, is swallowed up by the unstable floor like a modern-day victim of Pompeii.

In these large-scale images, the frontal confrontation with the body was intended to make the viewer more self-conscious and reflective:

I'm very interested in discord, that awkwardness, that I feel is so much part of real life. I want people not to be complacent, to feel slightly awkward. I think maybe too awkwardness makes you more aware of yourself as a viewer. As soon as you become a little bit more aware of yourself… you bring yourself into the equation and it's no longer this separate experience from your own body.

Drew speaks of another recent series, the *Still Life* series, in the same terms. Wary of repulsing people with her subject – native animal road kill - Drew sought to disarm the viewer by tenderly re-presenting the dead beasts within the familiar genre of European still life. While inviting an empathetic response to the animals through their transformation into offerings of food placed on a table, Drew subtly encourages a sense of discord or awkwardness. The grainy, rephotographed landscape backdrop of *Galah in Landscape* or the intrusion of the corner of the tablecloth in *Magpie with Pawpaw* function not as a reassurance that somewhere a landscape exists for the animals, but as discomfiting cues that they are terminally out-of-sync with it.

The cultivation of awkwardness, by which Drew means the
bringing of awareness back to the body, is characteristic
both of her approach to her photography and of the
affect she hopes it will produce in the viewer. It provides
a key to her explorations of landscape, understood as
a complex concatenation of the natural and industrial
worlds, myth, imagination, history, place and identity.
Rather than seeking to glorify or objectify "nature"
through the eye of the camera, still less master it, she
invites us to get to know landscape from the inside out,
to approach it in a spirit of humility, awe and playfulness,
to acknowledge our skewed and blunted humanity in
it, and through our awkwardness, to begin to address its
wounds.

Dr Caroline Jordan

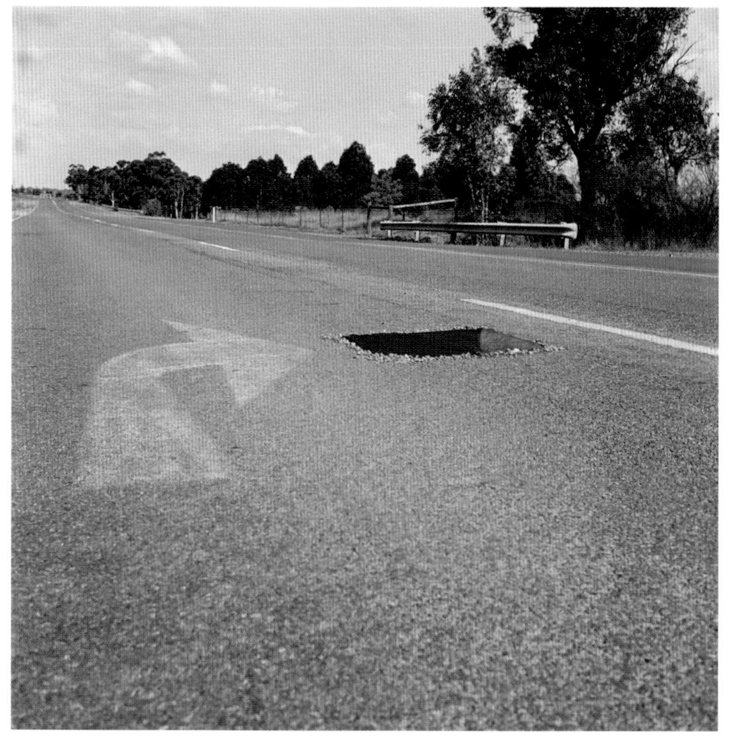

Hole 1 (1982)

Hole 3 (1982)

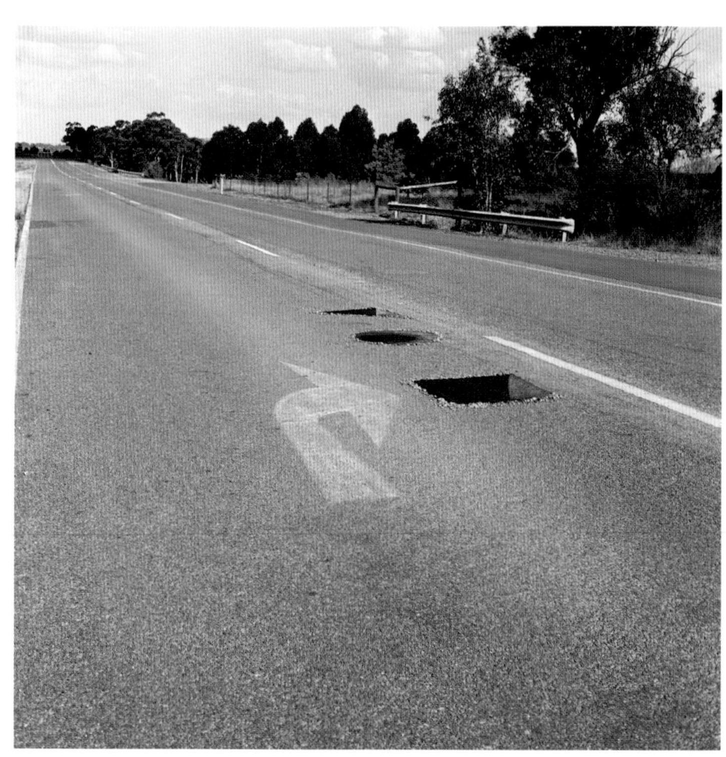

[1] All quotes are from an interview with the author, April 2006.

[2] J.G. Steele, *Aboriginal Pathways in Southeast Queensland and the
Richmond River*, St. Lucia: University of Queensland Press, 1984.

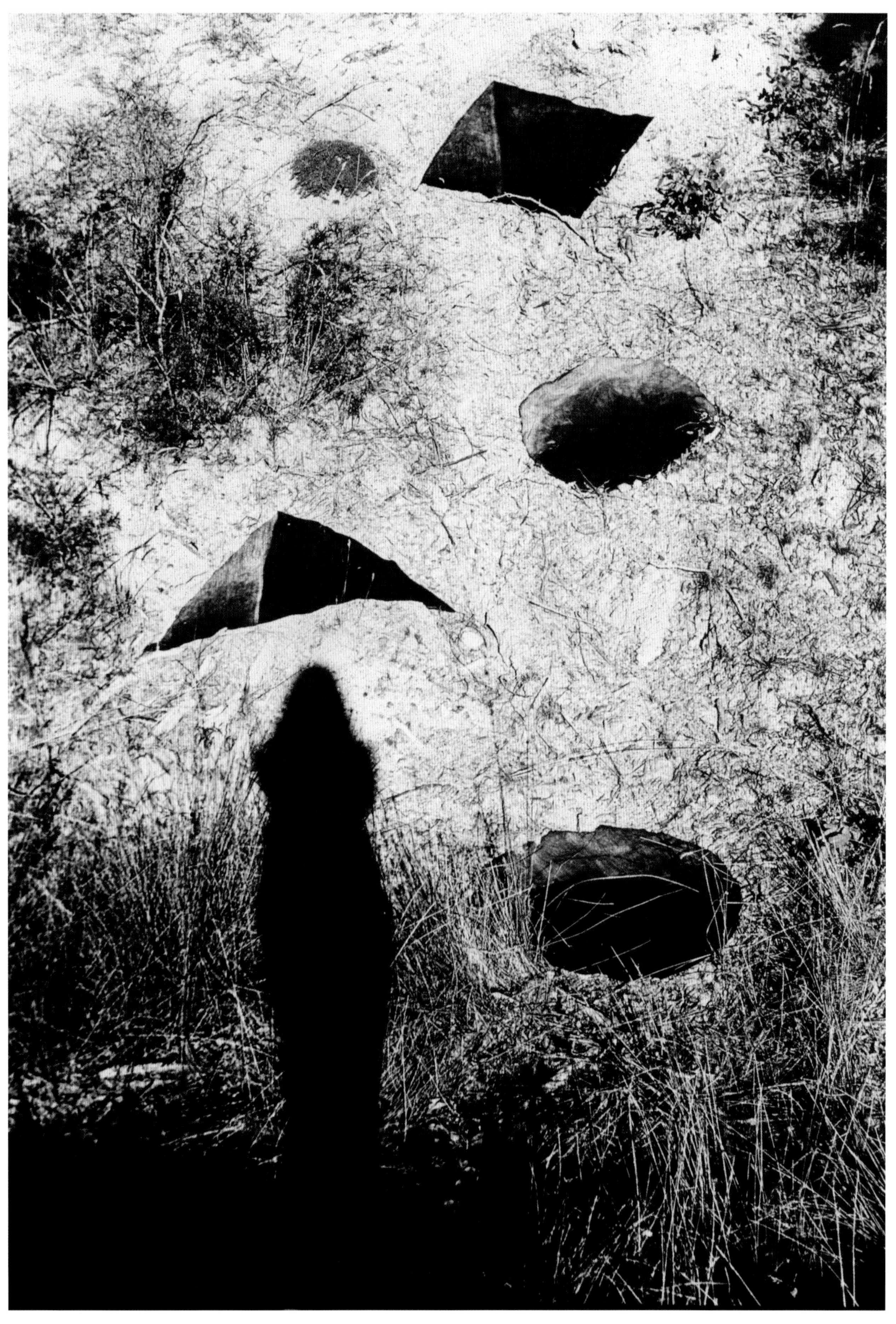

Untitled (1982)

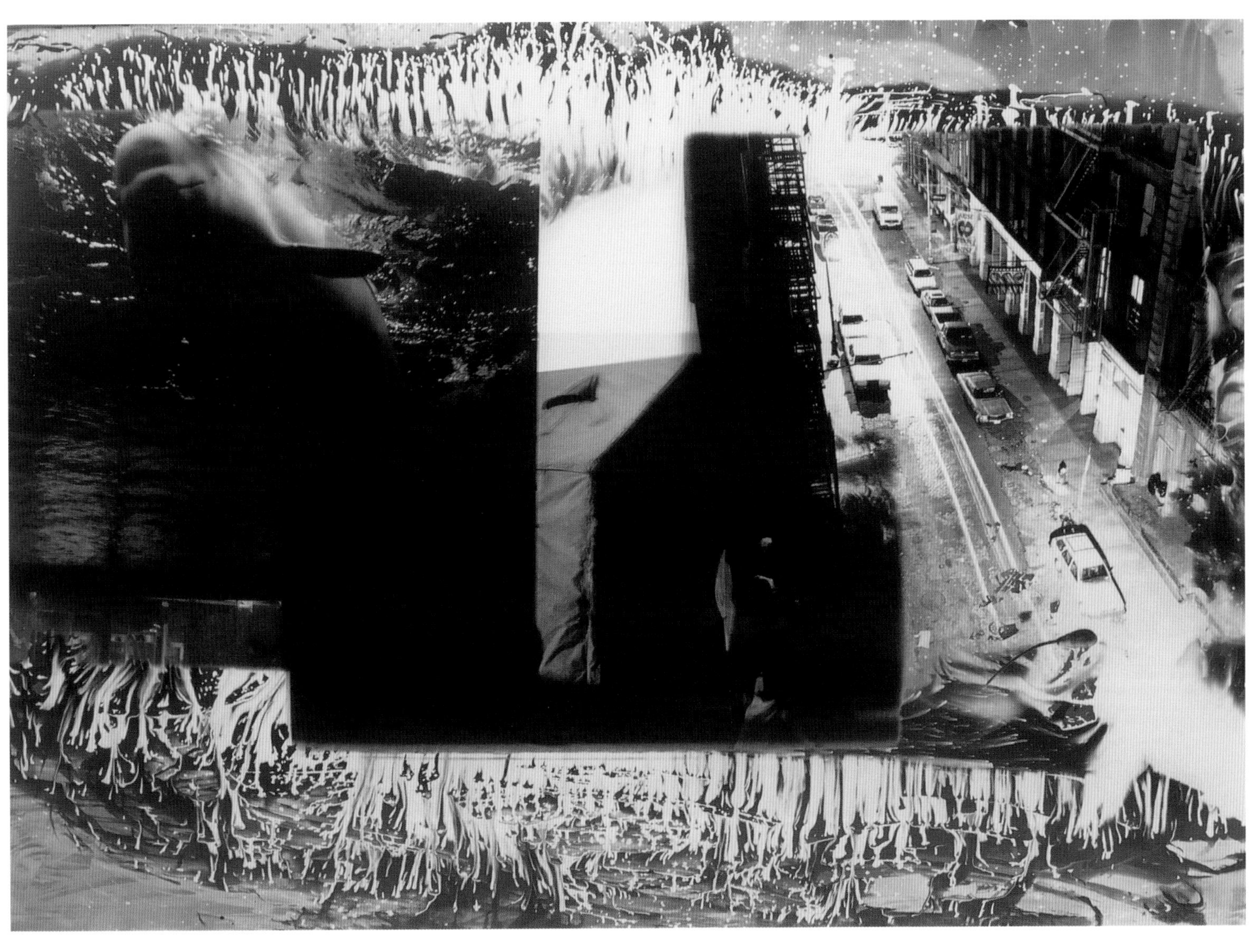

NY Aquarium (1997)

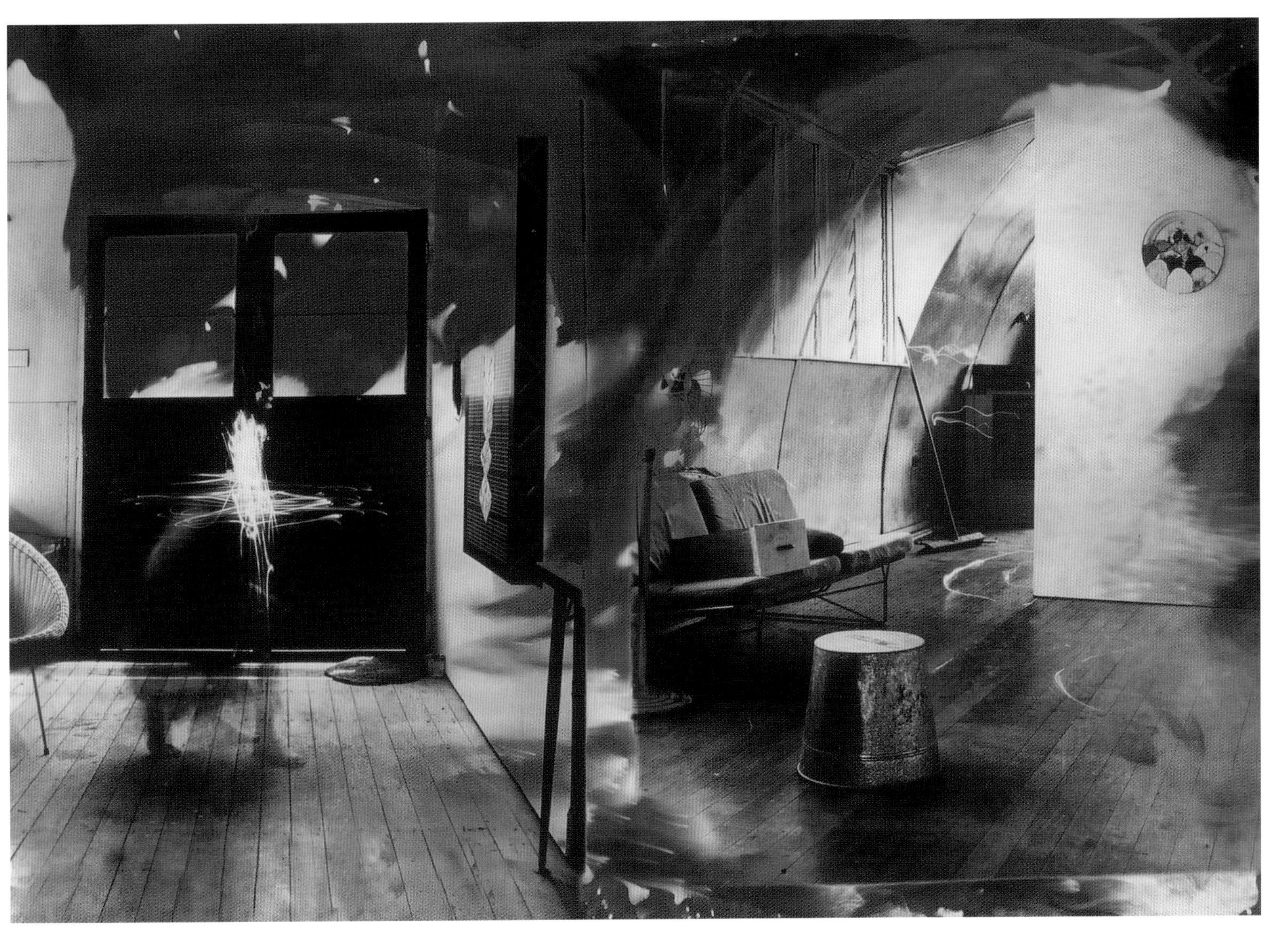

Studio landscape (1997)

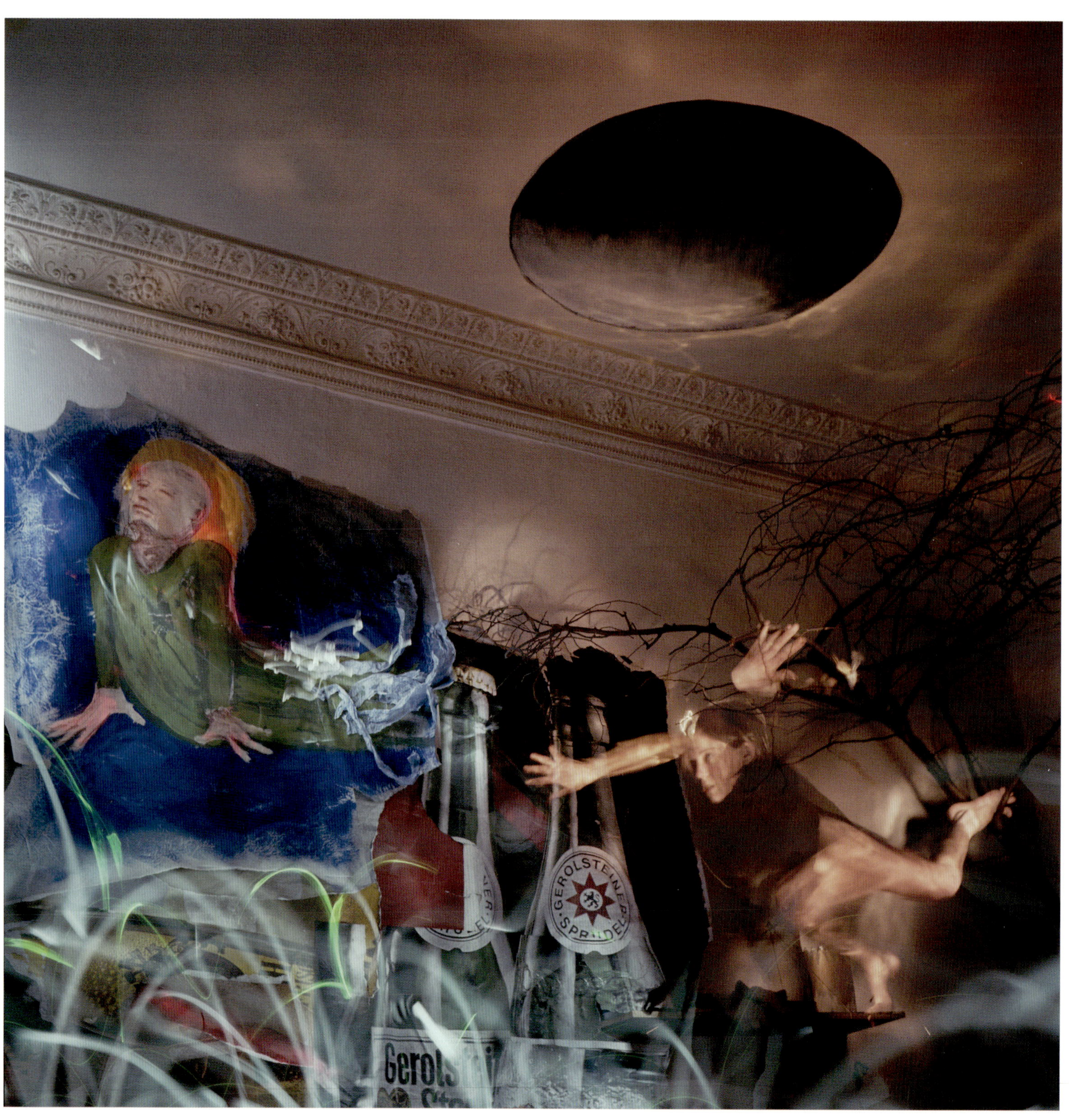

28   *One of four ways to fly (1) (1985)*

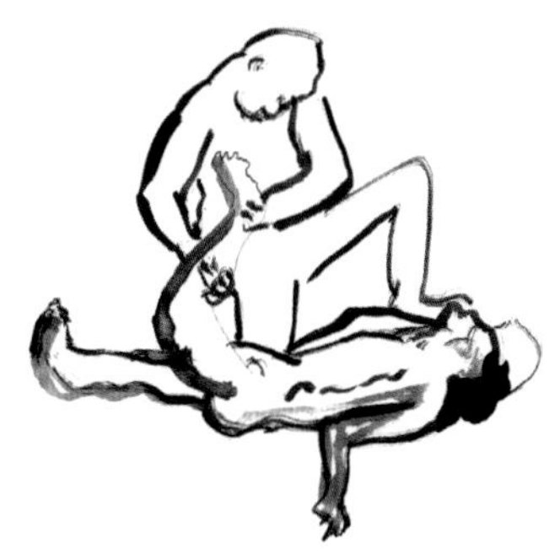

Turning the camera inwards:
Marian Drew's mysteries of the everyday (1986-96)

Prior to the 1970's, painting was up-held as innately superior to photography. Even during that era, when traditional canons of art production as a whole were interrogated and toppled, it would take a further decade to see a collapsing of the divide between the hand-made image and the mechanized. In Australia, this is when constructed tableaux became an identifiable force in camera work as much as "straight" photography and it was time when women artists found a medium that was young enough to be malleable.

The period addressed here takes account of Marian Drew's formal study in Canberra followed by a postgraduate course in experimental photography at Kassel Gesamthochschule, and Wynnum (an old, semi-rural suburb of Brisbane) where she resides with artist partner Bruce Reynolds. It examines the work resulting from her New York residency in 1989 and the four months she spent at the Australia Council studio in Santa Monica, Los Angeles, during 1995. Throughout these years, her "source" installations characteristically incorporated slide projection, collages of large drawings and patterned surfaces such as wallpaper, photographic prints and lights. If not directly including the body, human activity was always present in the resulting photomontages.

Majoring in photomedia at Canberra School of Art during 1980-84, Drew eschewed the mimetic tradition, experimenting instead with reality as a subjective, psychologically informed representation of experience. She metaphorically turned the camera inwards even though the lens faced outwards to the local landscape. On trunks of white gums, painterly marks, newspaper text, close-ups of white picket fences from suburban homes were projected from slides. With this series of *Bush projections*, Drew tackled white man's claiming of country.

In her student period, the performance art of Jill Orr and Stelarc impressed her and she recalls that 'the main photography I was seeing were documents of performances and way-out events'.[1] Orr had already articulated the naked body for the camera in *Bleeding Trees* (1979) and Stelarc was pursuing his suspension works in Australia and overseas. Drew brought traces of the body (more often than not her own) into photo-work during the latter half of the 1980's and early 90's. This was not to record the body under duress or to link

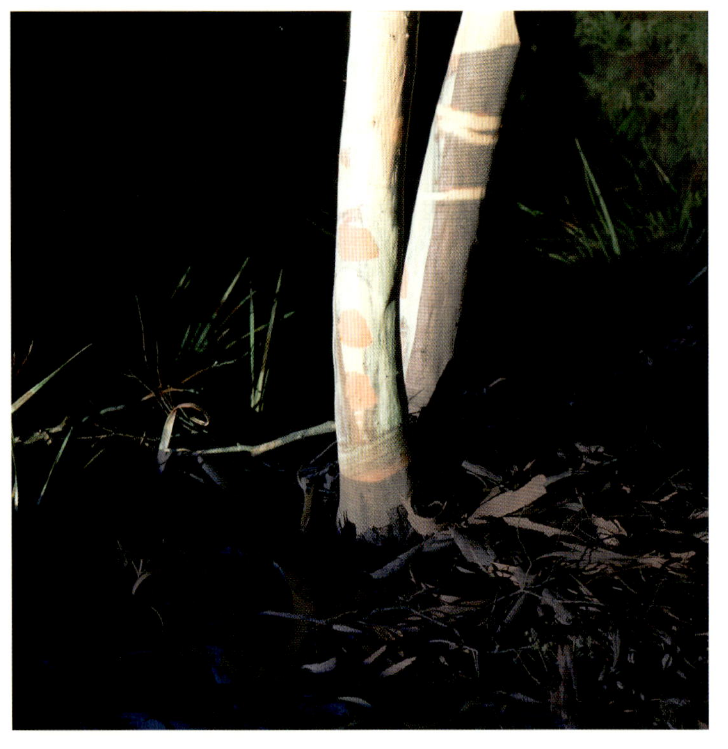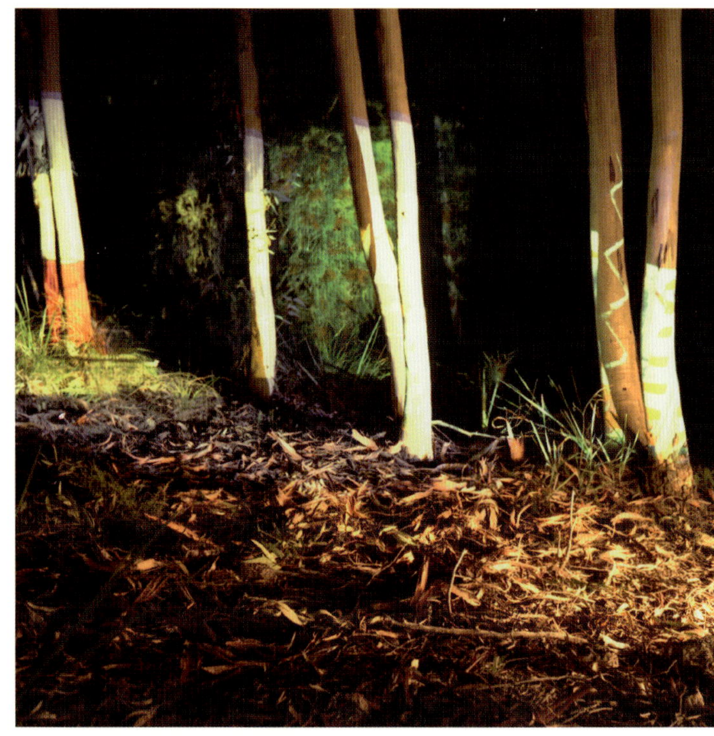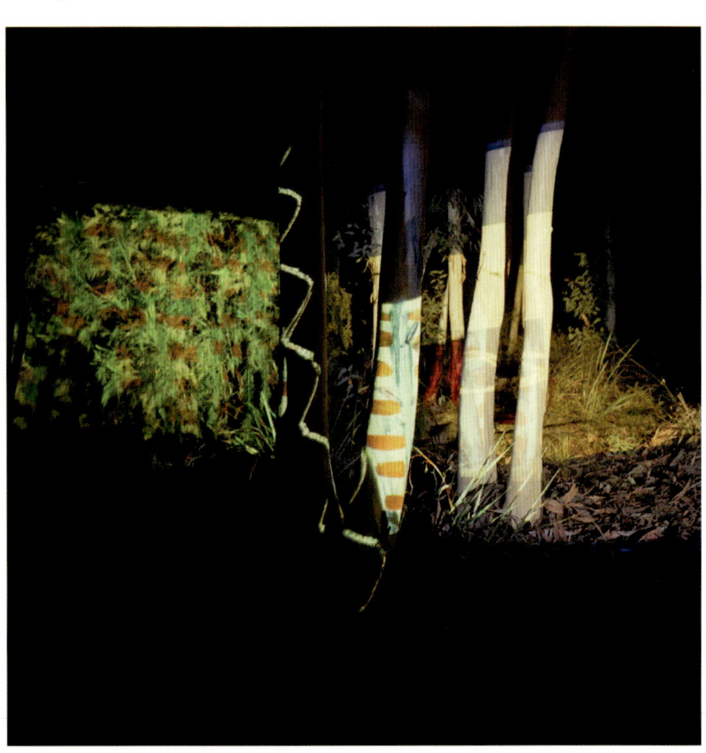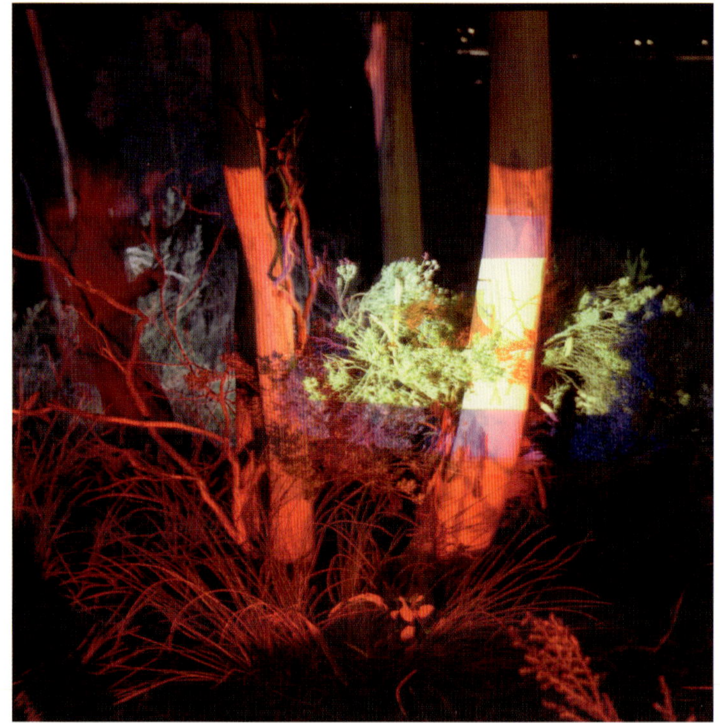

 opposite and above: *Untitled, Bush Projections* (1983)

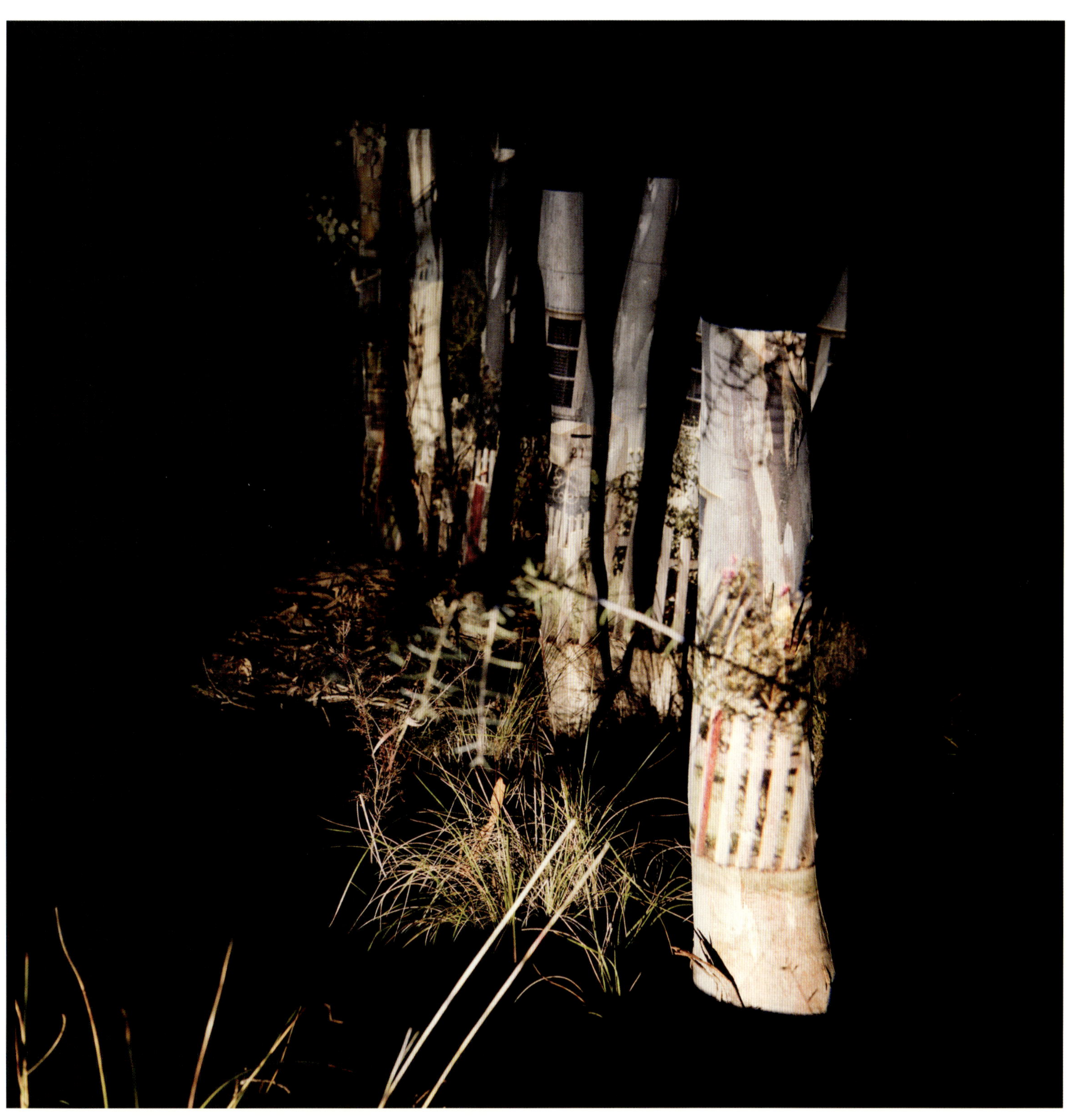

it to environmental issues, but to indicate the human presence in her richly complex images. The imagery was a barometer of where she was living and what was preoccupying her at the time.

In the second half of the eighties, Drew's home in Wynnum became the stage for photographs which fused a new-found engagement with Queensland, with domesticity and interpersonal relationships. Two of these works were purchased by the Queensland Art Gallery soon after they were made in 1987. Printed by the artist in an edition of ten, they are modest in scale yet ambitious in composition and intention. *Cabbage and bowl* was not simply a still life but a statement in reaction to the photograph being perceived as the result of a single viewpoint, a perception that implied 'the frame, the photographer as a secret voyeur... I wanted instead to let the whole scenario kind of evolve in an unplanned way.' Drew has always been attracted to the futurist photographers who conveyed sensations of movement and the surrealists with their uncanny distortions, and both their influences were apparent here. She incorporated her drawings in this work as soft painterly mark-making on paper sheets scattered beneath the cabbage and portion of meat. In the left margin, she introduced her face with a hand over the eyes as if to stress the importance of the unconscious. The domestic theme continued in the second work *The dance 1* (originally titled *The argument*). Here, two figures in frenzied contrapuntal movement are contrasted with the staid interior of an old Queenslander home.

The artist's images became increasingly complex during the six month period she spent in New York, with the continued use of long (fifteen minutes or more) exposures allowing for the construction of subjects from blurred movements, slide projection and by "painting" with torches of various colours and lights. Drew often incorporated herself, or Reynolds, sometimes a rough-drawn biblical figure borrowed from Masaccio, or other masters of European art, as well as references to Asian deities. The dense urban situation she was experiencing, with its anxiety and unpredictable Virilio-like ethos, contributed to these highly charged photographs. *Late Fall* (1989), also from the Queensland Art Gallery collection, sums up the *New York* series well. The naked falling figure, reminiscent of the Inferno sequence of Dante's Divine Comedy, is surrounded by a maelstrom of drawn and painted props, newspapers and studio debris. This is a nocturnal, downtown metropolis. Drew

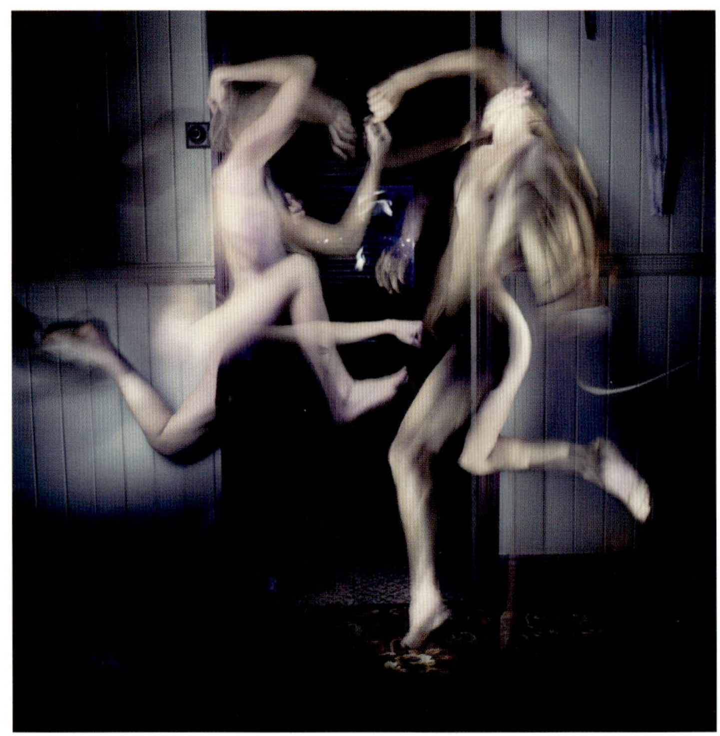

The Dance 1 (The Argument) (1988)

The Dance 2 (1988)

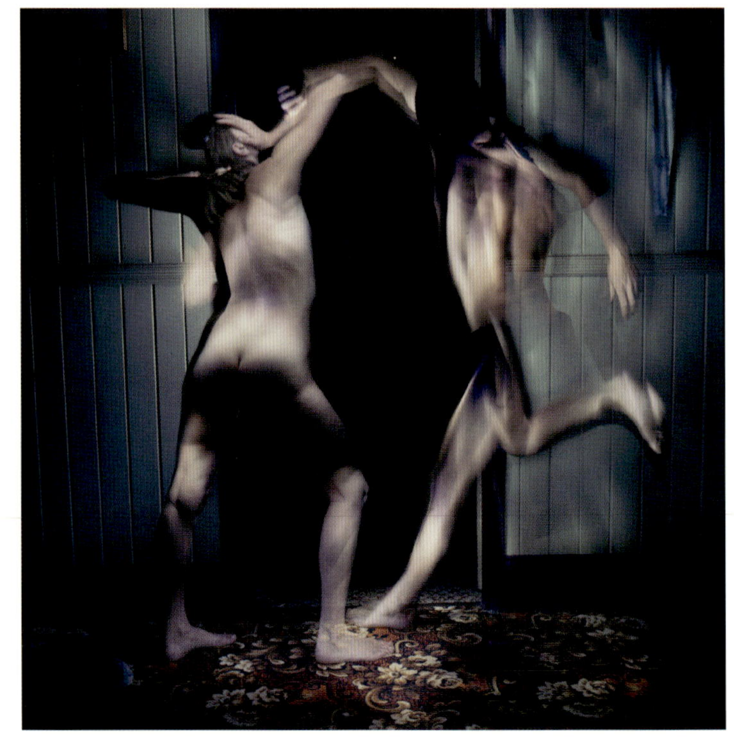

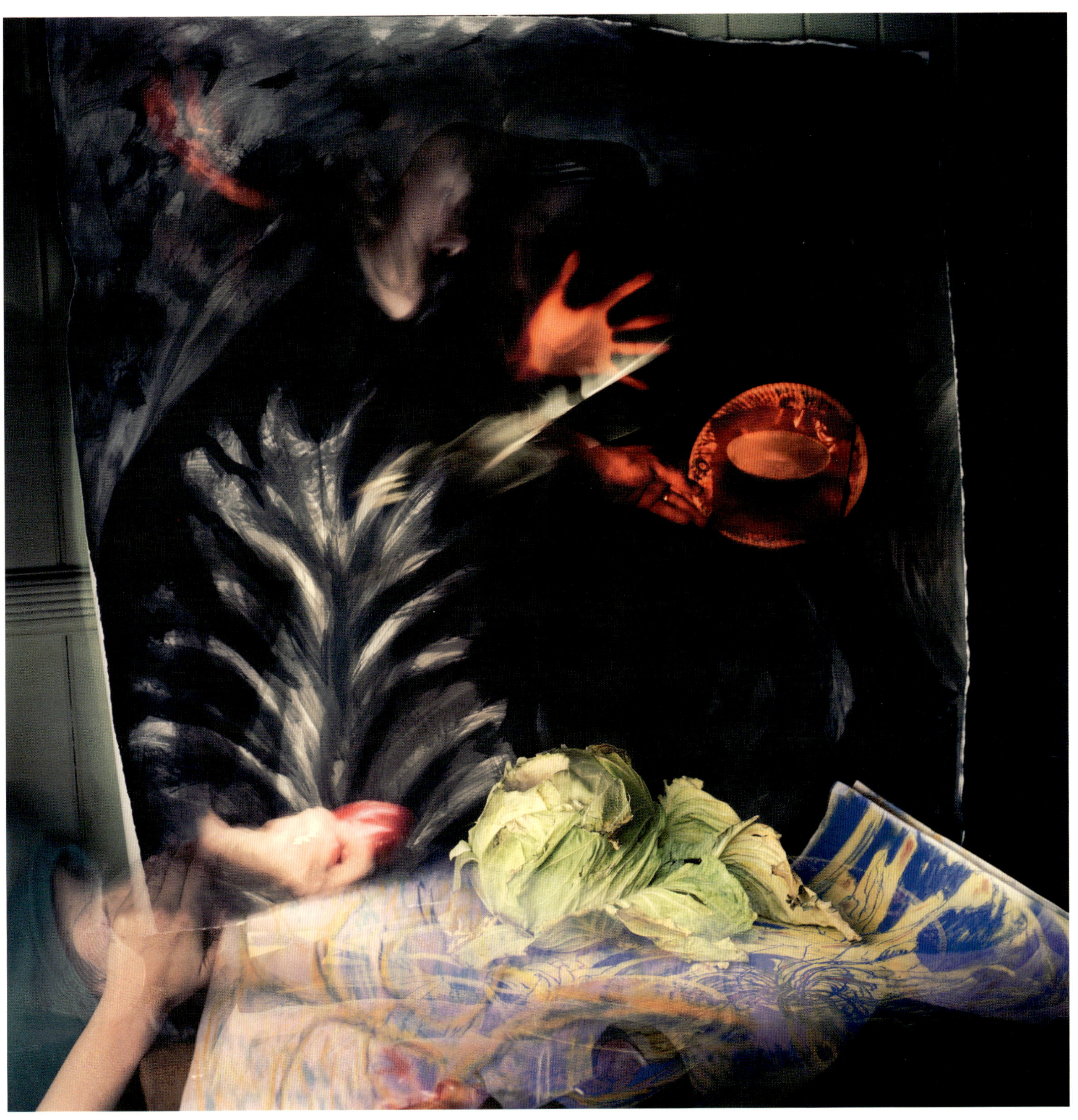

Cabbage and bowl (1988)

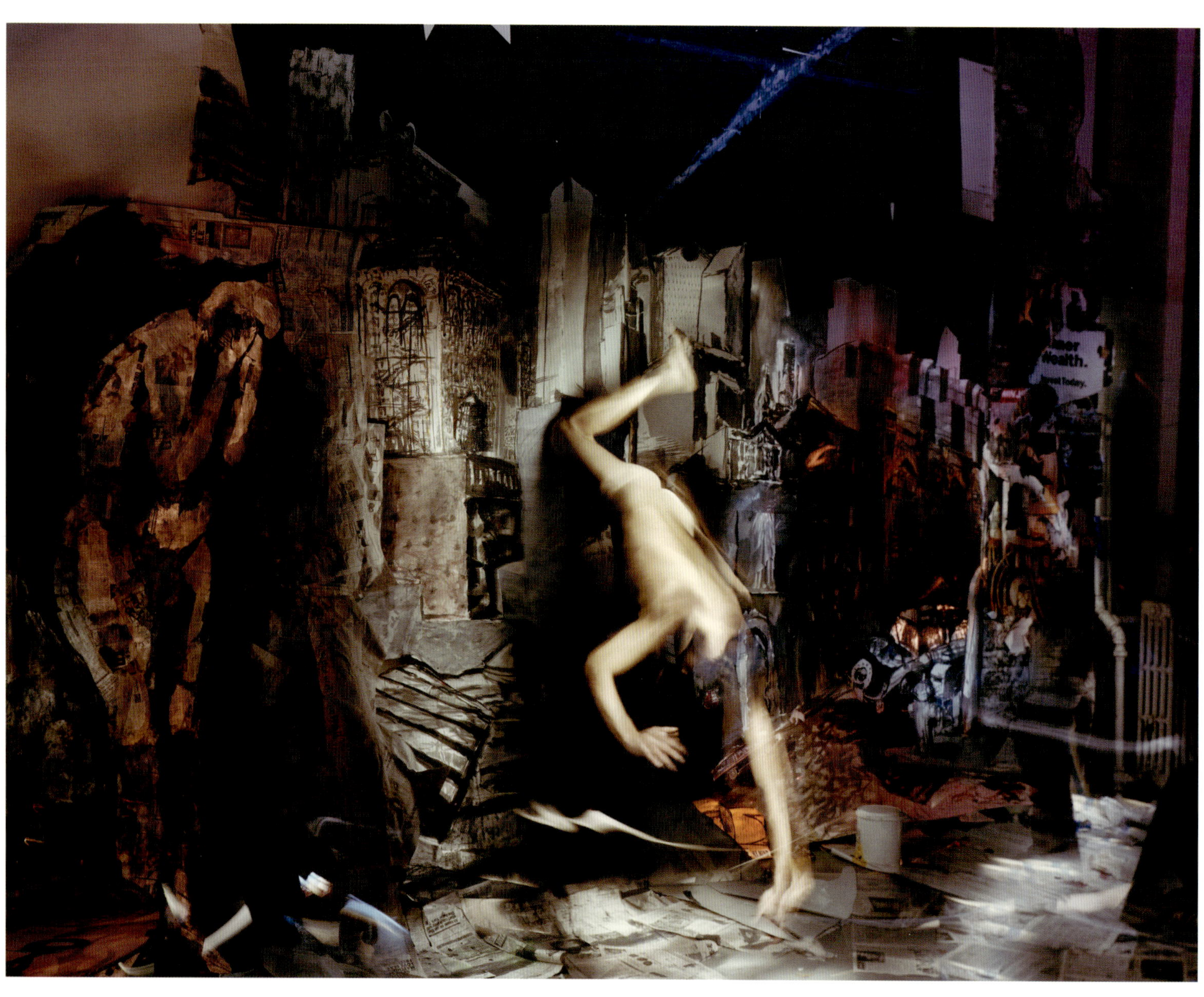

34   *Late Fall* (1990)

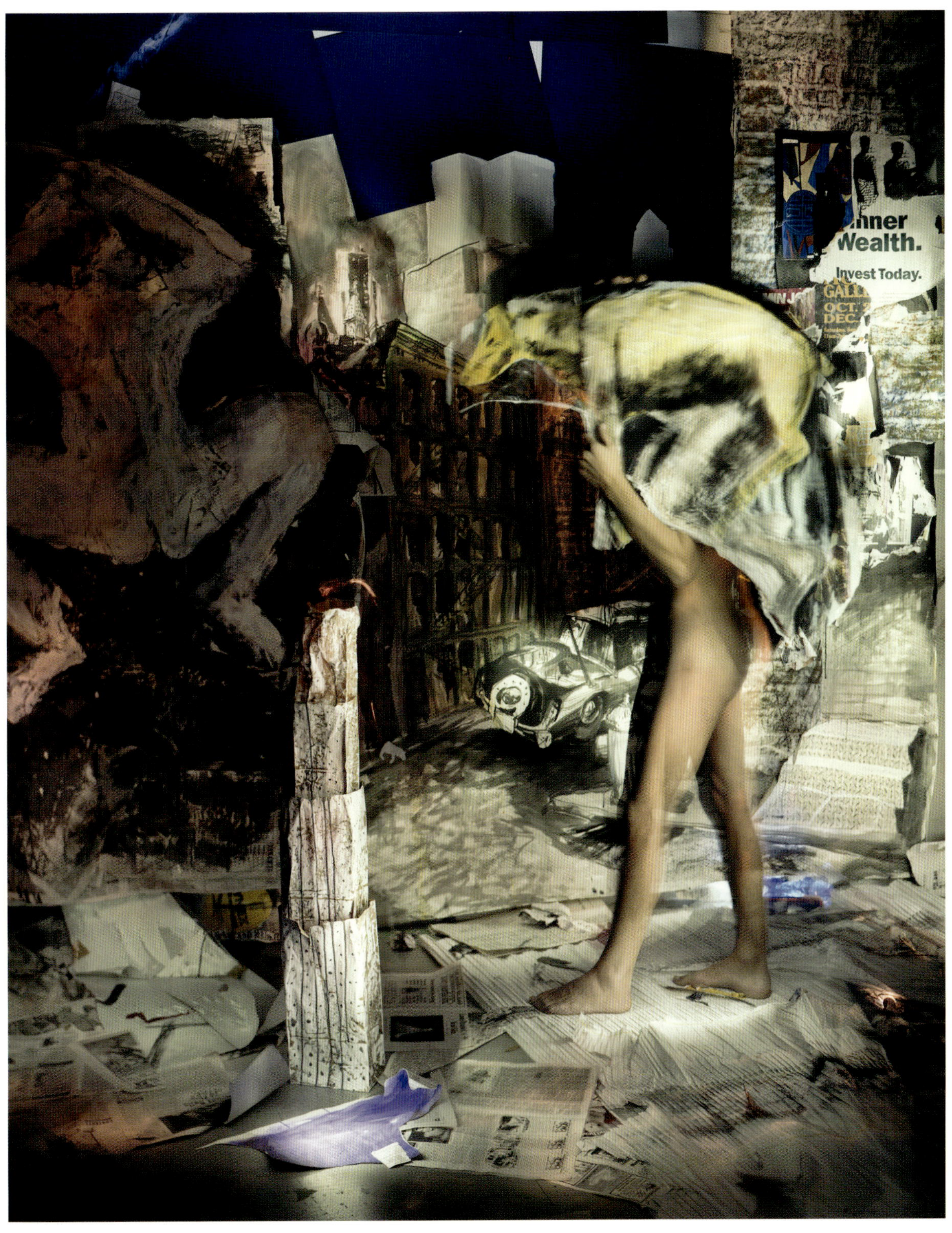

Animal interference (1990)

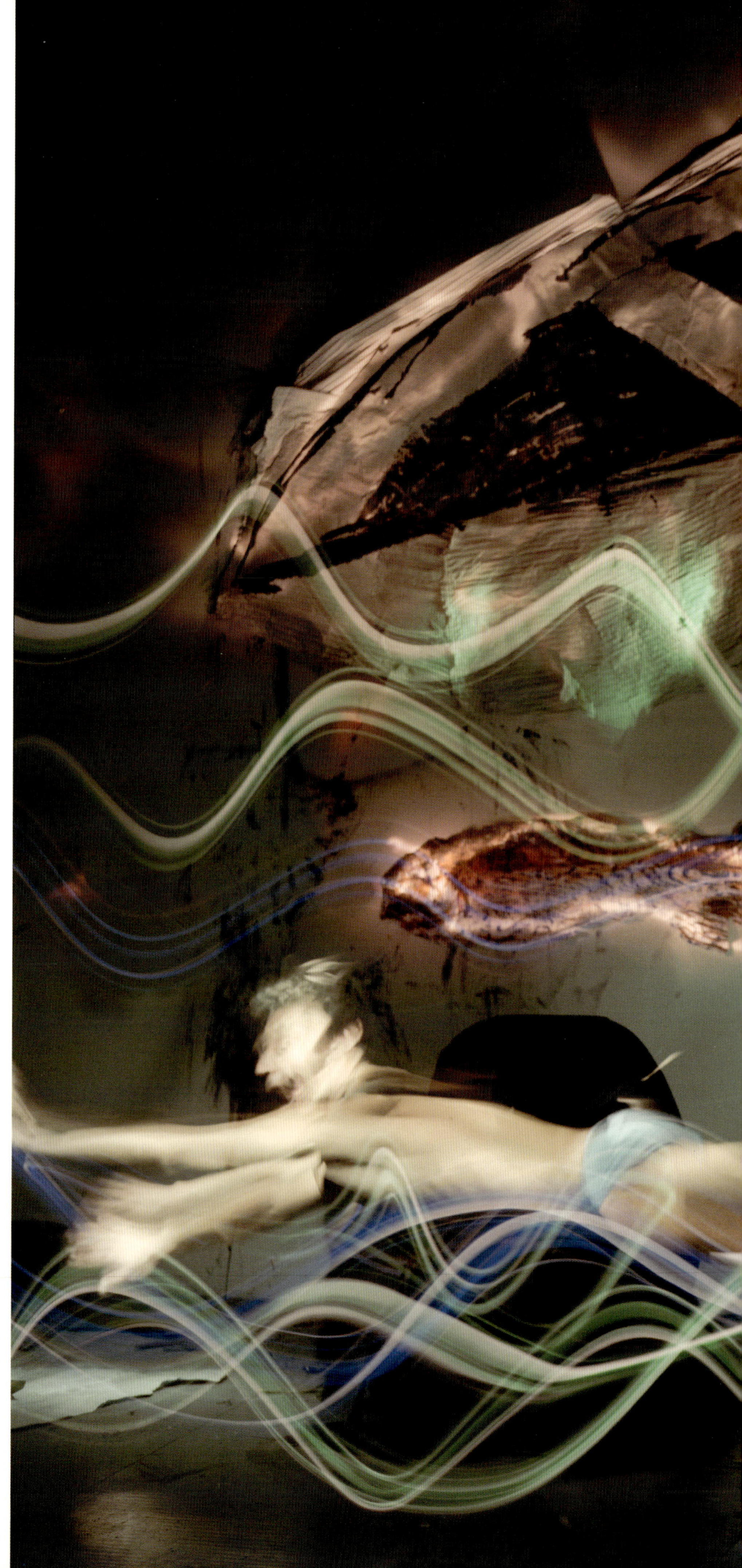

36   *Boats with swimmer* (1990)

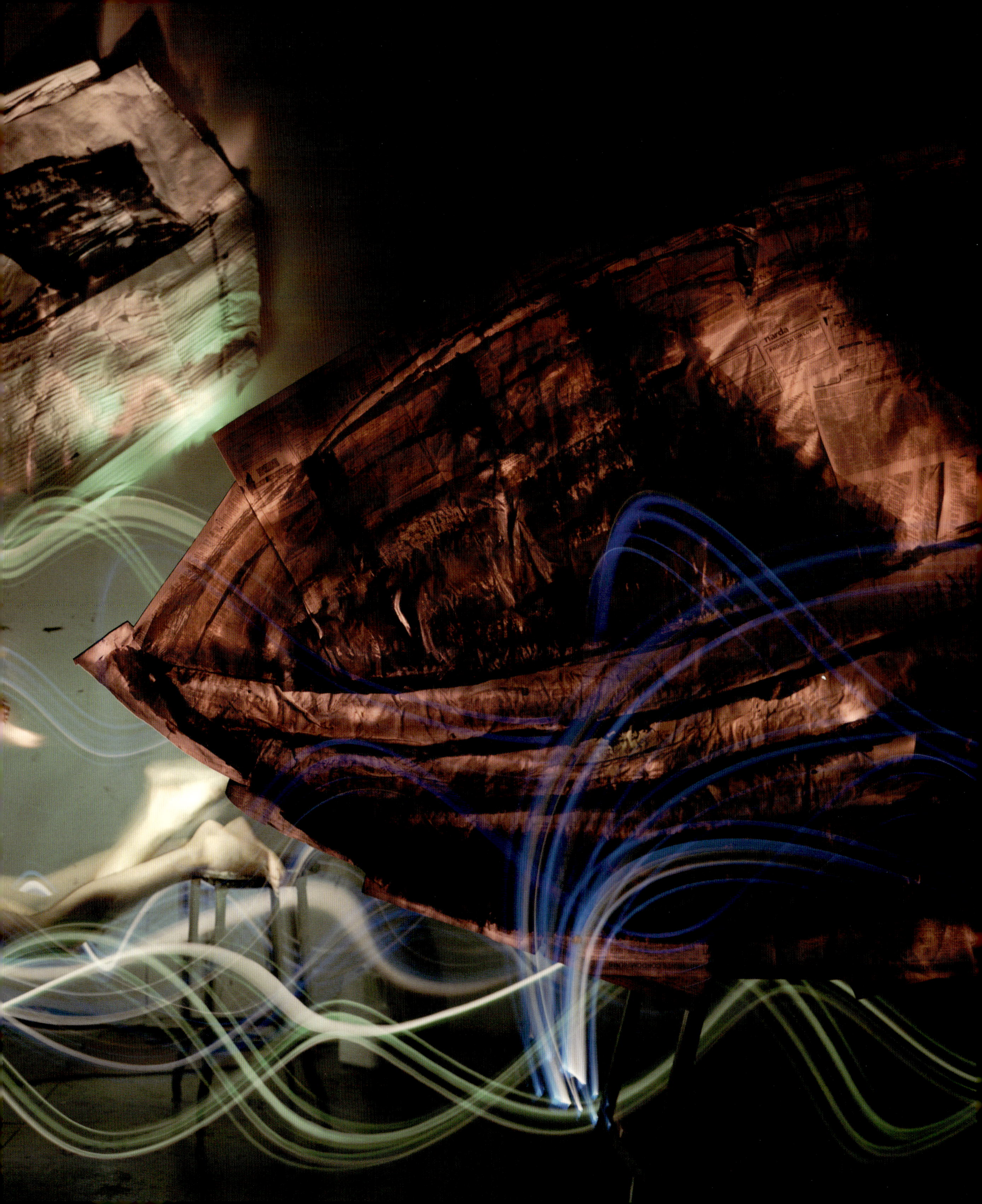

recalls 'working in New York was intensely emotional, lots of images surfaced, bubbled up in this stimulating city. The above ground, and the below ground, I had a strong sense of this …it was Dickensian to me and psychologically dream-like.'

Of the *New York* works Clare Williamson has written of the paradoxical painterly quality of these large Type C photographs and of the performative process where Drew charts the energy of passing time within each composite image.[2] A photograph from the series in the artist's possession, is a version of *A beautiful and enduring myth* (1990-93) and is marked by the absence of the figure, yet retains the memory of that presence. Staged in a large industrial shed (a studio on Drew and Reynold's property), a block on which he/she has crouched a moment before, links the body with the column of hand drawn figures plunging in Dantesque formation to supposed purgatory. Strong primaries – blue, yellow and red – are painted with house-brush sweeps in rough geometry on a paper backdrop or provided through artificial lighting. This is photography that gives power to the invisible through dramatic staging and risk taking, which plays out the artist's belief that 'concrete reality is a construction… your own projection as opposed to just being stable and out there'.

Drew realigned her approach to photography at about the time she was appointed artist-in-residence at Sommerville House girl's school, Brisbane, in 1993. Technically the photographs continued to be the same, with vibrant colour and large-scale formats, yet there was increasingly an interest in symbolic ritual and how spirituality can be expressed as an implicit part of the individual and, in turn, of the community. From her base in Wynnum, Drew had started researching early colonial histories of the area and later revisionist accounts. She became interested in the artefacts of non-Western cultures as well as the history of Australia's indigenous peoples and their deep respect for the natural environment. In *Paper and rock* (1992) the blurred figure of the artist confronts a palimpsest of drawings and collaged illustrations from early Queensland texts. She thus implicates herself with the ancient practice of rock art by Aborigines and documents of their disturbing past under European settlement.

Marian Drew's photography has never exploited the glossy "mechanical" nature of lab-produced images

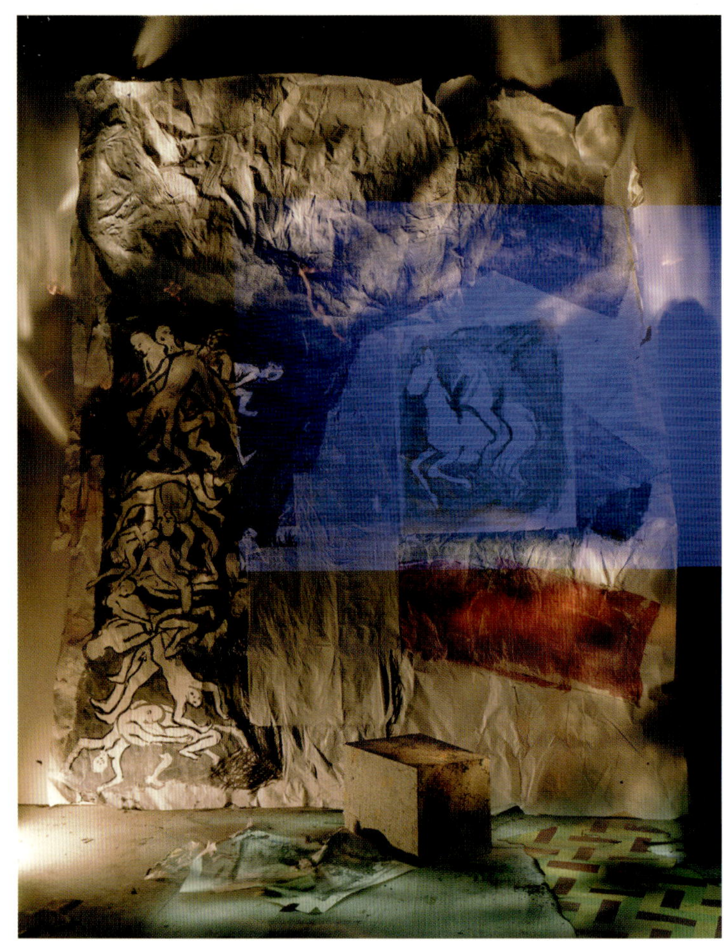

*A beautiful and enduring myth
(with blue light) (1993)*

   opposite: A beautiful and enduring myth (1993)

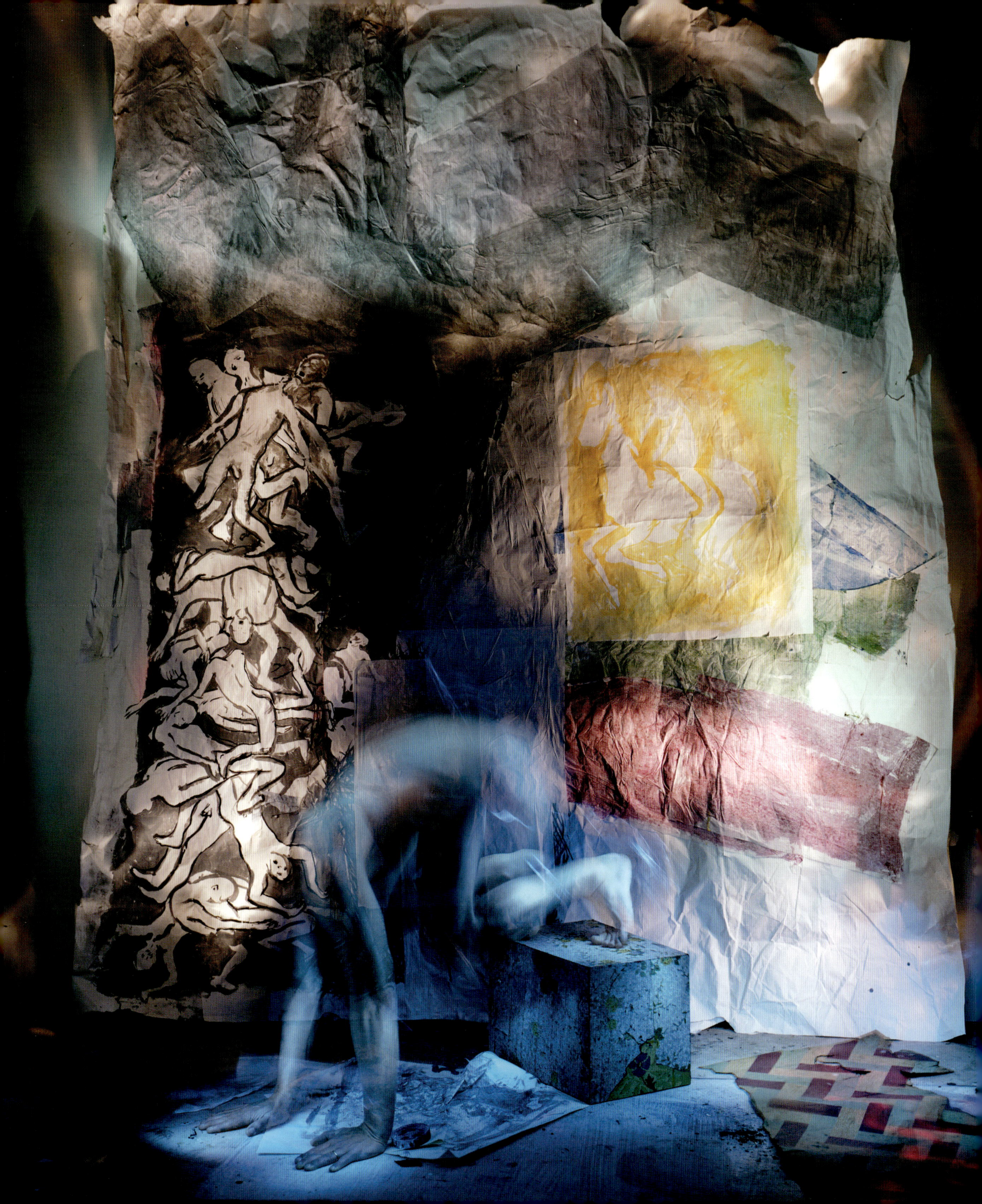

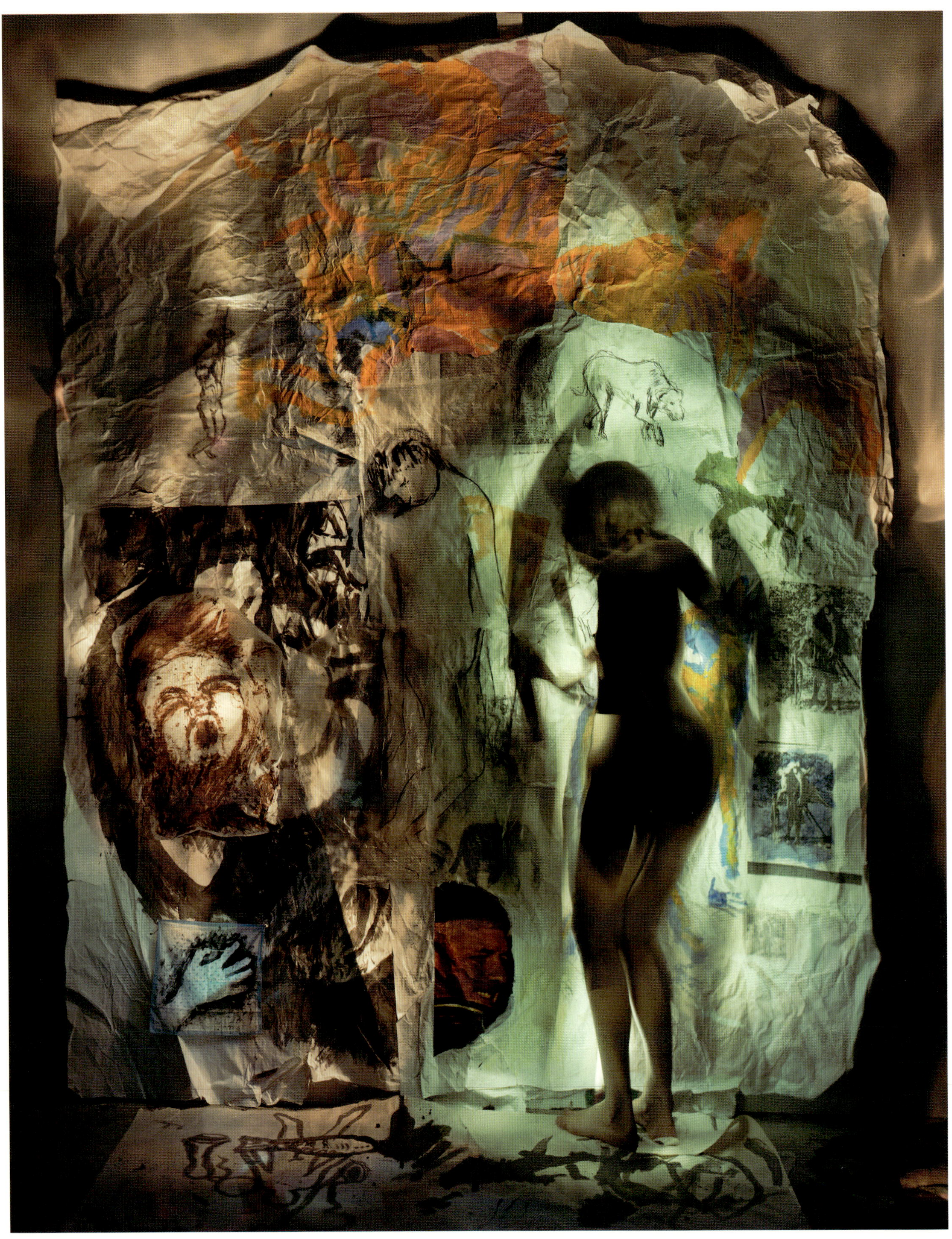

   Paper and rock (1993)

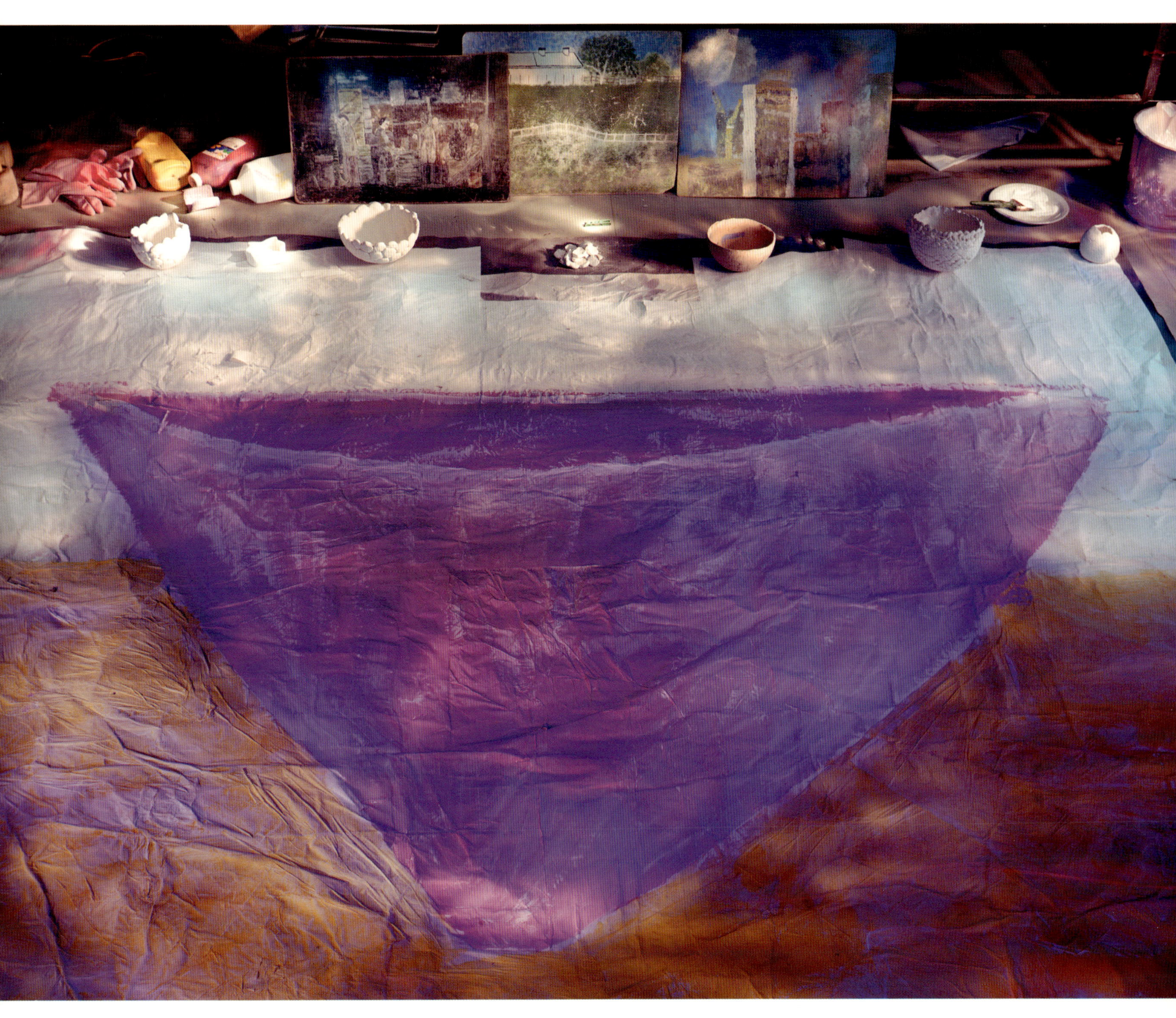

over the language of autographic gesture. What she achieves in her practice is a creative tension between two seemingly irreconcilable realms. The trace of the hand and obvious evidence of physical production in her imagery continued to be significant during the early nineties, informed by her circumstances. As a mentor at Sommerville, Drew produced, among others, the photograph *Crude and cumbersome objects frozen into place* (1993). She recollects that 'by collecting imagery like the crude clay vessels, the student paintings used as clay boards, a drawing made with paint and tissue paper, I involved these objects, made or found, in a situation of introspection, participation, play and construction that seeks new relationships and meanings for the objects. Film welds the passage of time with place; recording the paths and variations of light as the objects are defined.' The motif of the vessel with its associations of sustenance and female sexuality stand for the body in this photograph and give it both tangible and intangible weight.

When Drew travelled to Los Angeles with Reynolds and their young children, she found herself making small sculptures in clay (and borrowing those of her daughter) in much the same way that she had previously used the drawing process: to initially explore ideas. Deliberately funky and awkward, these objects appeared out of the rituals associated with family life in the Californian context. Through necessity, she pared down her practice to focus on the creativeness of the untutored mind and the bathos of domesticity. Small clay figures, a baby's bottle and other objects entered her photographs as totems for this period of her life. 'The rawness was important in these objects, their unselfconsciousness…I was interested in elevating these clumsy objects, to make them important… and to also record those accidents occurring in daily life, accidents that may seem trivial, like when you spill milk, but which may also be profound'. In this series of works exhibited under the title of 'Persistent Blindness' at Brisbane City Gallery in 1996, the handmade artefact became a surreal protagonist in her pictures, often accompanied by trails of light and the clutter of the kitchen sink.

A departure from the earlier photographs was the simplification and clarification of these images. They took up where *Crude and cumbersome objects frozen into place* left off. Previously Drew had explored space by physically moving the body through found and

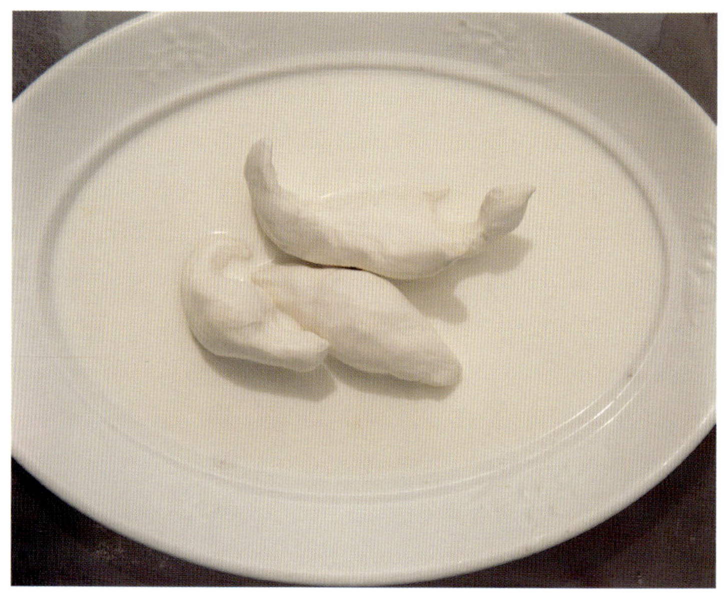

Clay and milk (1996)

Tree and milk (1996)

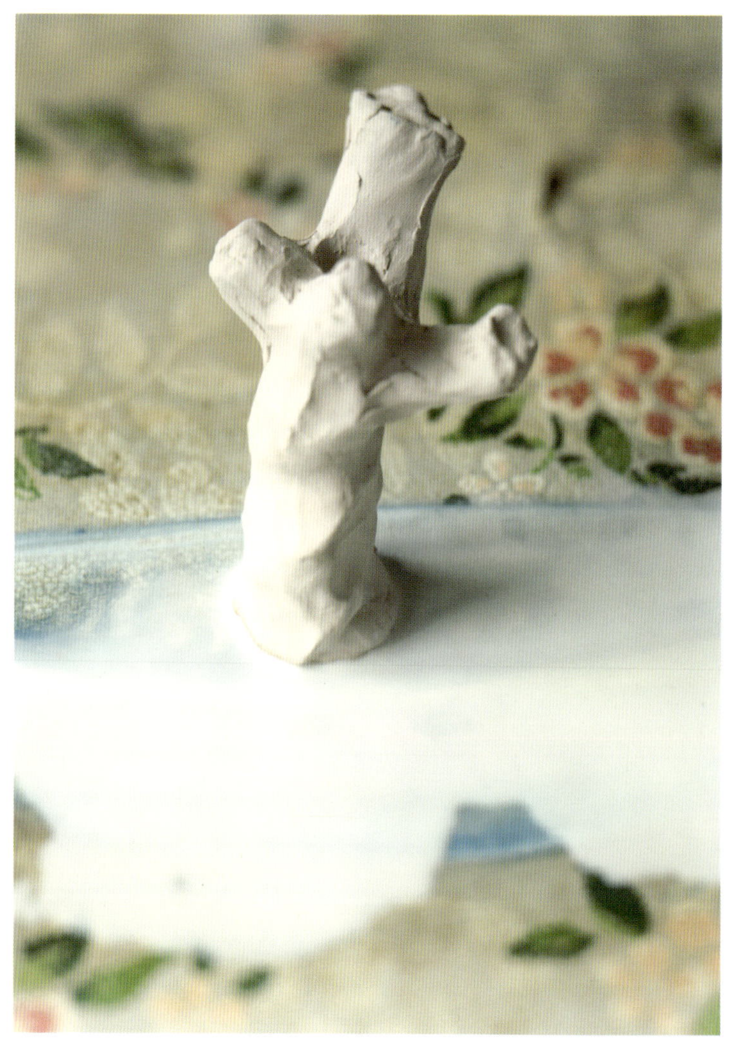

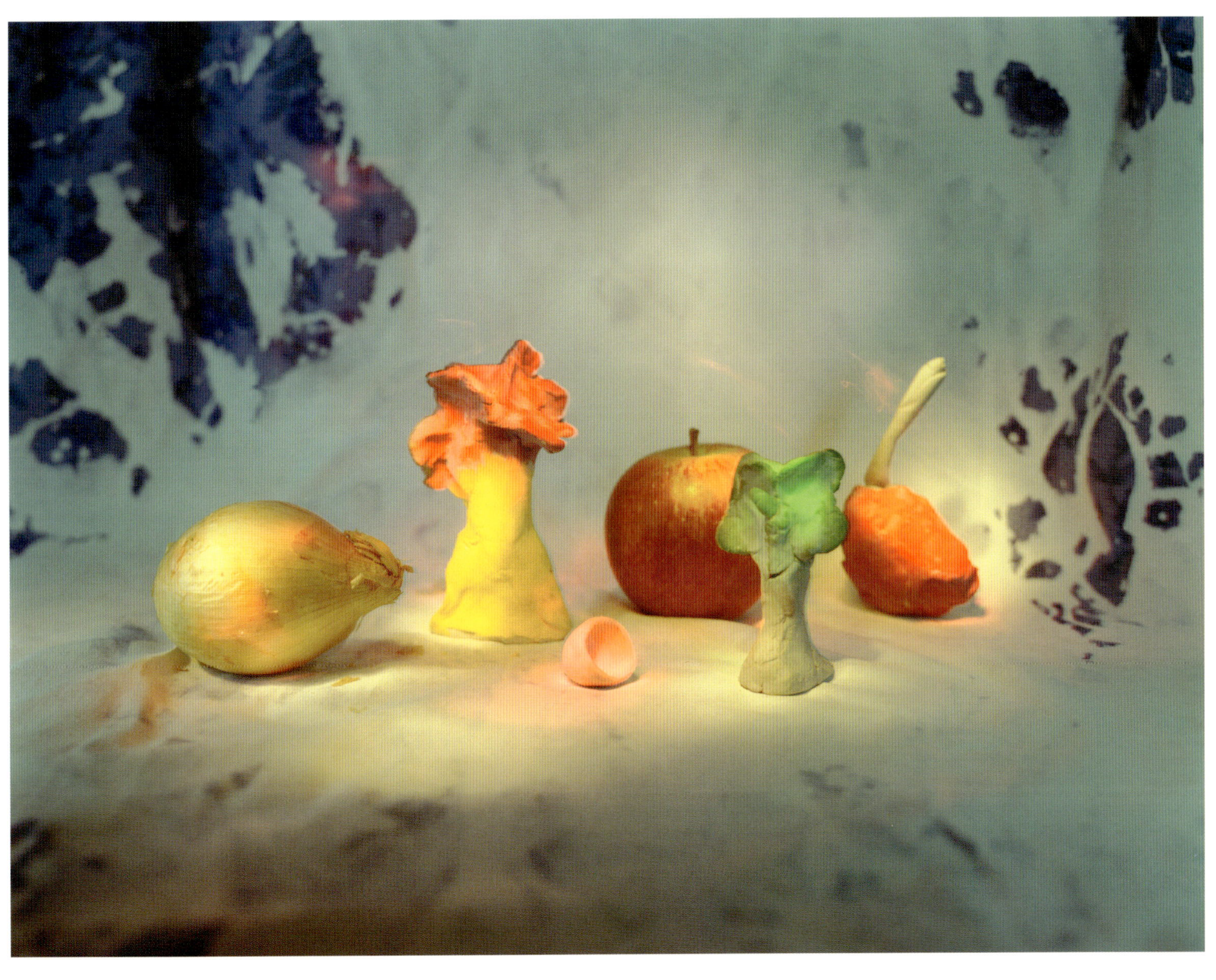

Still life with clay trees (1996)

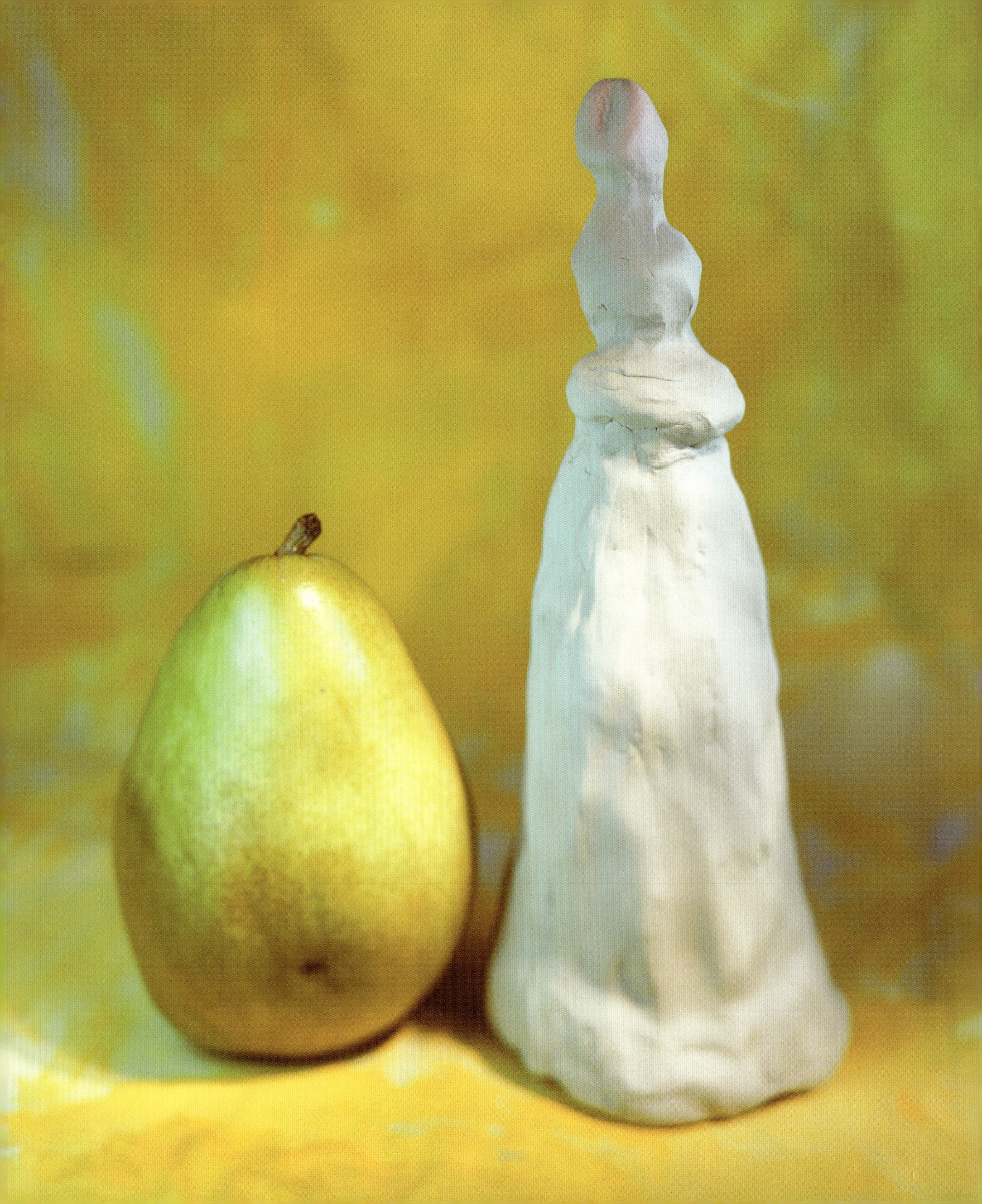

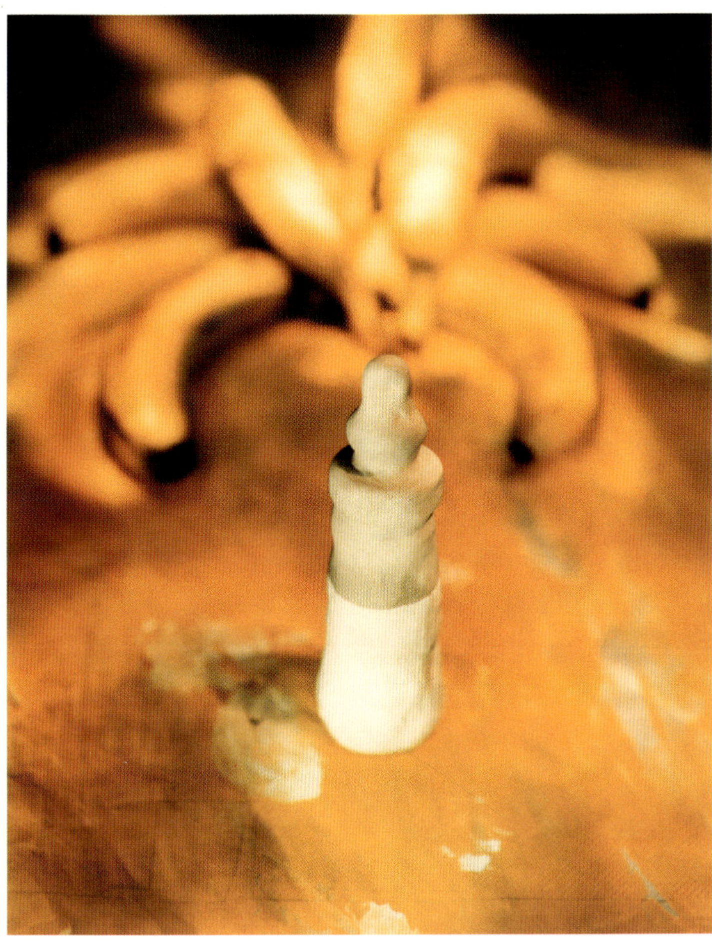

Untitled (1996)

[1] Marian Drew in conversation with the author, 9 February 2006. All quotes are from this source or from a recorded conversation between the author and Marian Drew, 1 June 1996, in preparation for the artist's solo exhibition 'Persistent Blindness' at Brisbane City Gallery later that year,

[2] Clare Williamson, 'Painting illusion or photographic reality?', essay in *Marian Drew: New York series*, The Queensland College of Art Gallery, Brisbane, 2-27 April 1990.

constructed props, leaving a light trail or blur to mark the human passage. With the Los Angeles-inspired work, she re-phrased pop art by selectively photographing collages made from lengths of patterned fabric, children's kennel club appliqués and magazine cut-outs. In this claiming of the quotidian domain as central to her practice, the humble pumpkin and potato became part of her repertoire. Her inventiveness in juxtaposing found materials with the ungainly little clay objects (enlarged far beyond their original size), engaged the viewer very directly. The brilliant, unpredictable talent of Sigmar Polke and his refusal to be typecast in his productions is perhaps the most useful comparison with Drew at this point in her career. (She had seen a major retrospective of this artist at the end of her Californian sojourn). Objects lumpy and threatening yet sustaining (such as the potato), clashing patterns and unresolved edges, luminous and beautiful passages, superimposition of one image over another, are points of resemblance which Drew shared with the German artist.

The decade of 1986-1996, witnessed Marian Drew creating a personal history though engaging with the particular here and now in which she found herself, at turns mundane and eventful. As the Surrealists proposed in the 1920's, she liberated "the marvellous" from conventional reality, giving the quotidian a magical and at times, wry and humorous twist. But she also addressed the underbelly of Australia's colonial past, the turmoil of a large metropolis and the dark side of the soul. At the vanguard of Queensland's postmodernist photography, Marian Drew felt no compulsion to neglect her love of drawing, or her attraction towards high-keyed colour and incorporated both as a photographer in a decade of highly productive practice. What was of paramount importance to her was 'seeking within my own immediate environment, the archaic in the present and the heroic in the everyday.'

Anne Kirker
Senior Curator (Special Projects)
Queensland Art Gallery

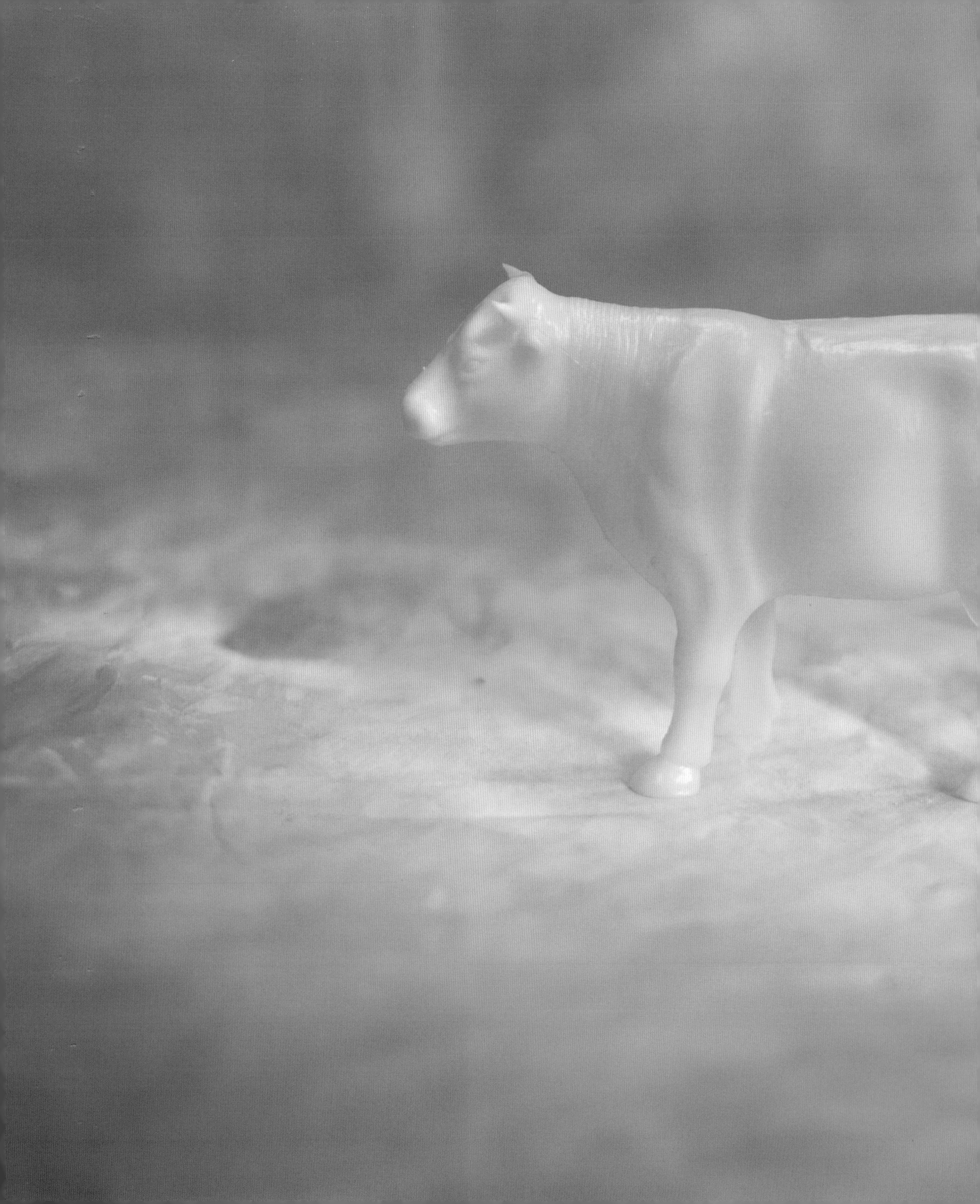

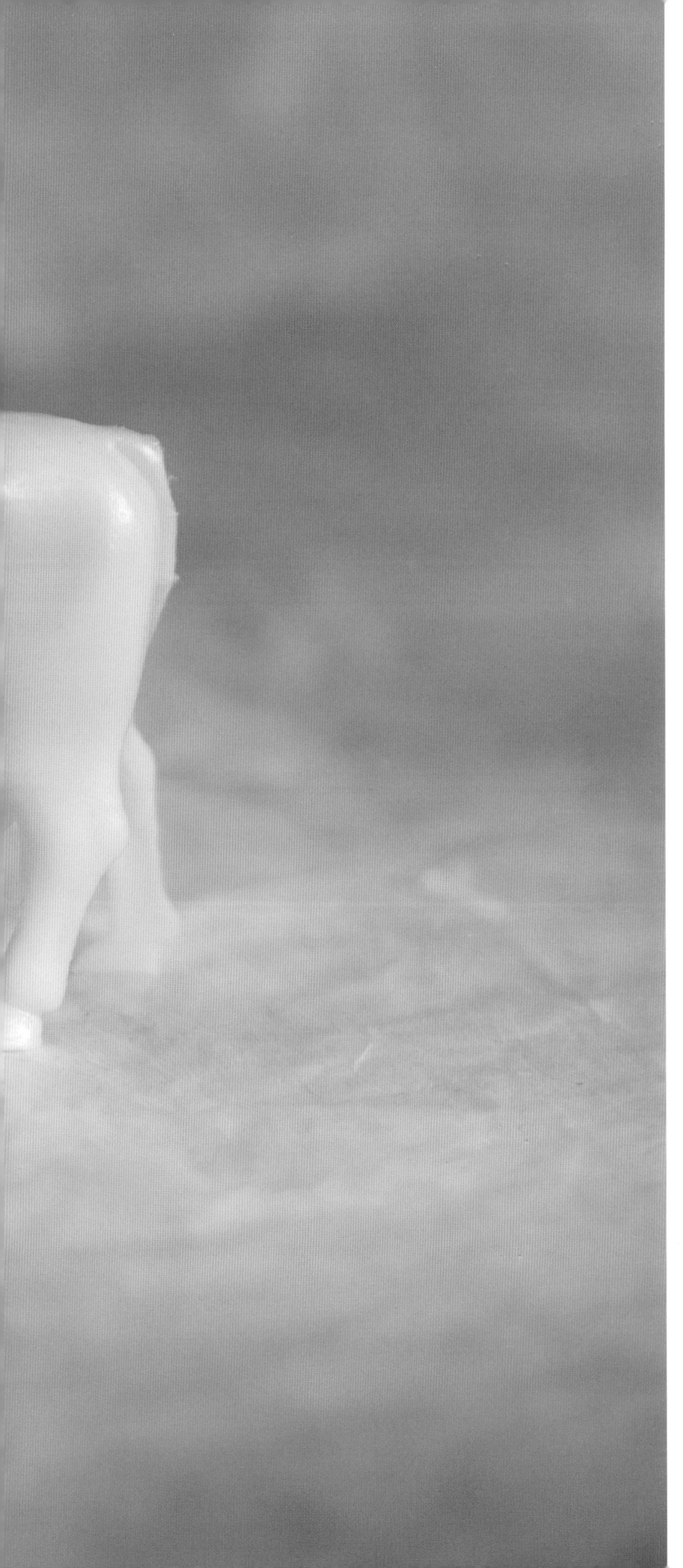

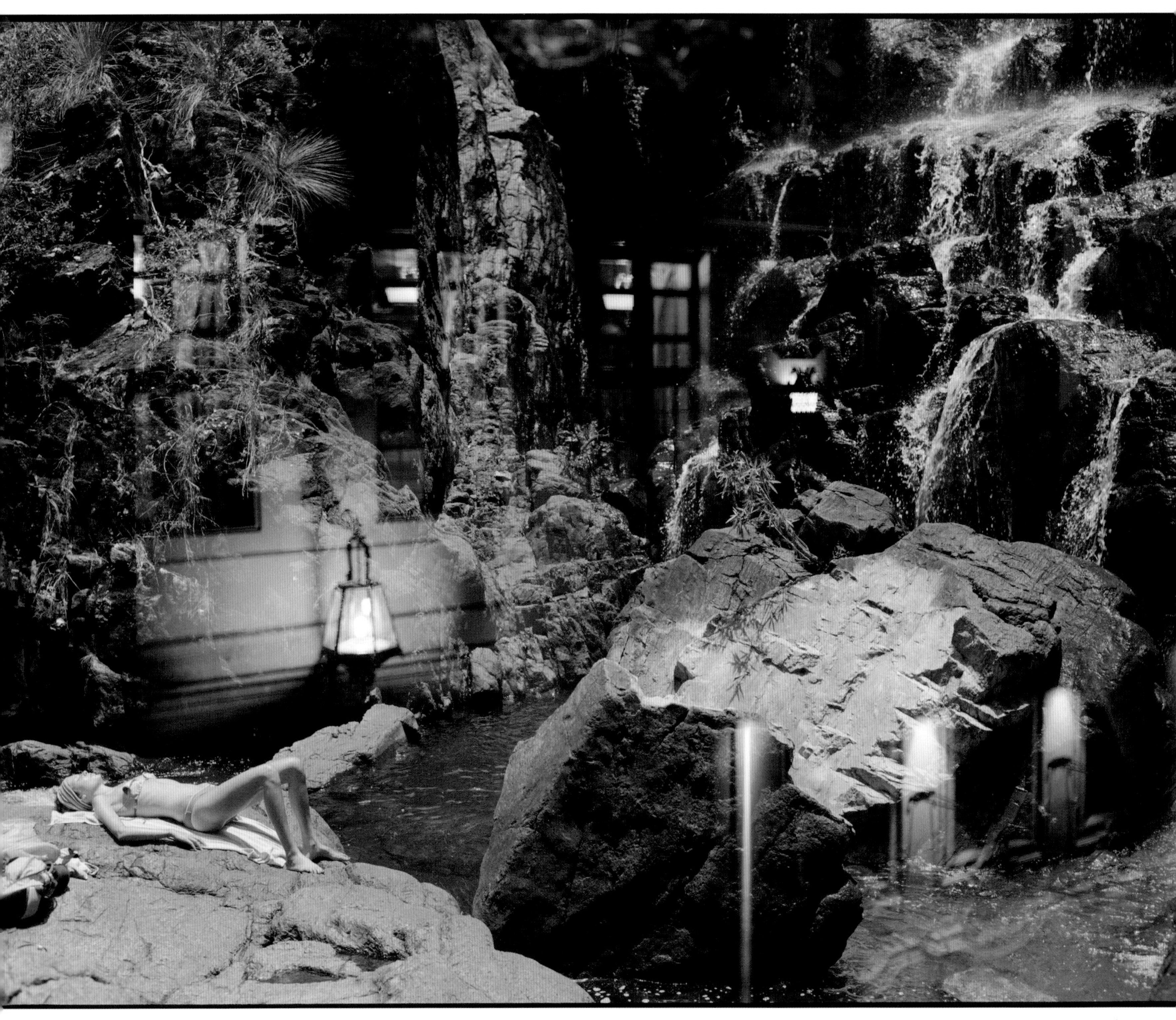

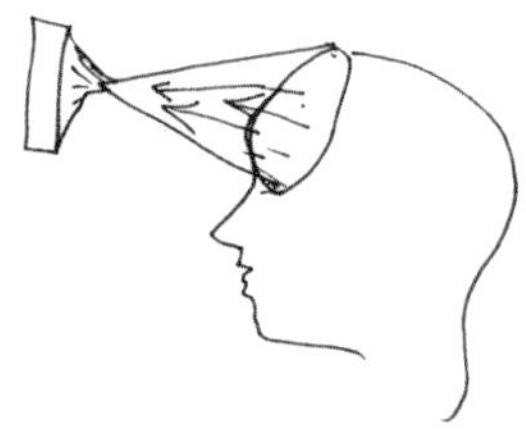

Awake / Asleep

In photography we see nothing. Only the lens 'sees' things. But the lens is hidden. It is not the Other which catches the photographer's eye, but rather what's left of the Other when the photographer is absent. We are never in the real presence of the object. Between reality and its image there is an impossible exchange. (Baudrillard, 'Photography: or the Writing of Light')[1]

Photography has always entranced its viewers with its particular promise of materiality, its signification flickering between index and icon, at once a trace and a verification of something real. However the medium does not secure a position or a perspective of sight; instead we are left with 'what's left', the residue not of the Symbolic order but of light itself. In this sense, photography bears witness to light's dispersal, its flow across objects and worlds in what feels like a moment, as the all-at-once impact of the hand on the camera inaugurates the 'instantaneity', the tactility, of the photographic image.

Such residue's of light can be clearly discerned in Marian Drew's series of long exposure works, *Light Matter* (1999), where family forms lined up in the darkness seem to

have been bleached onto the film. These forms bespeak no perspective beyond their own quotidian intimacy, and the images constitute a shift of vision away from photographer towards the photographic mechanism, into the body of the camera. We can also trace this light more closely in Drew's photogram series *Pond Life* (1998) and *Tank Stream* (2004), where the photographer's own labour with flowing water and light sensitive paper rather than her seeing eye mediates her relation to the picture. Between 2001 and 2005 Drew produced, collaboratively with German artist Thomas Bachler, a series of photographic double exposures entitled *Awake /Asleep*. This series engages with the materials and practices of time through the mechanics of the photographic image and processes, the intricate ways photographic technologies at once promise and render impossible a faithful reproduction of reality, presenting us with the coincidence of a world that appears to be both visible and real. In this, for Baudrillard the photograph is 'apophatic', working to keep silent 'what cannot be said', rather than 'epiphanic', and the photographic act generates 'intimate complicity' between the camera and the world rather than tangible or indeed singular 'mastery'.[2] This manoeuvre is of course at the heart of all

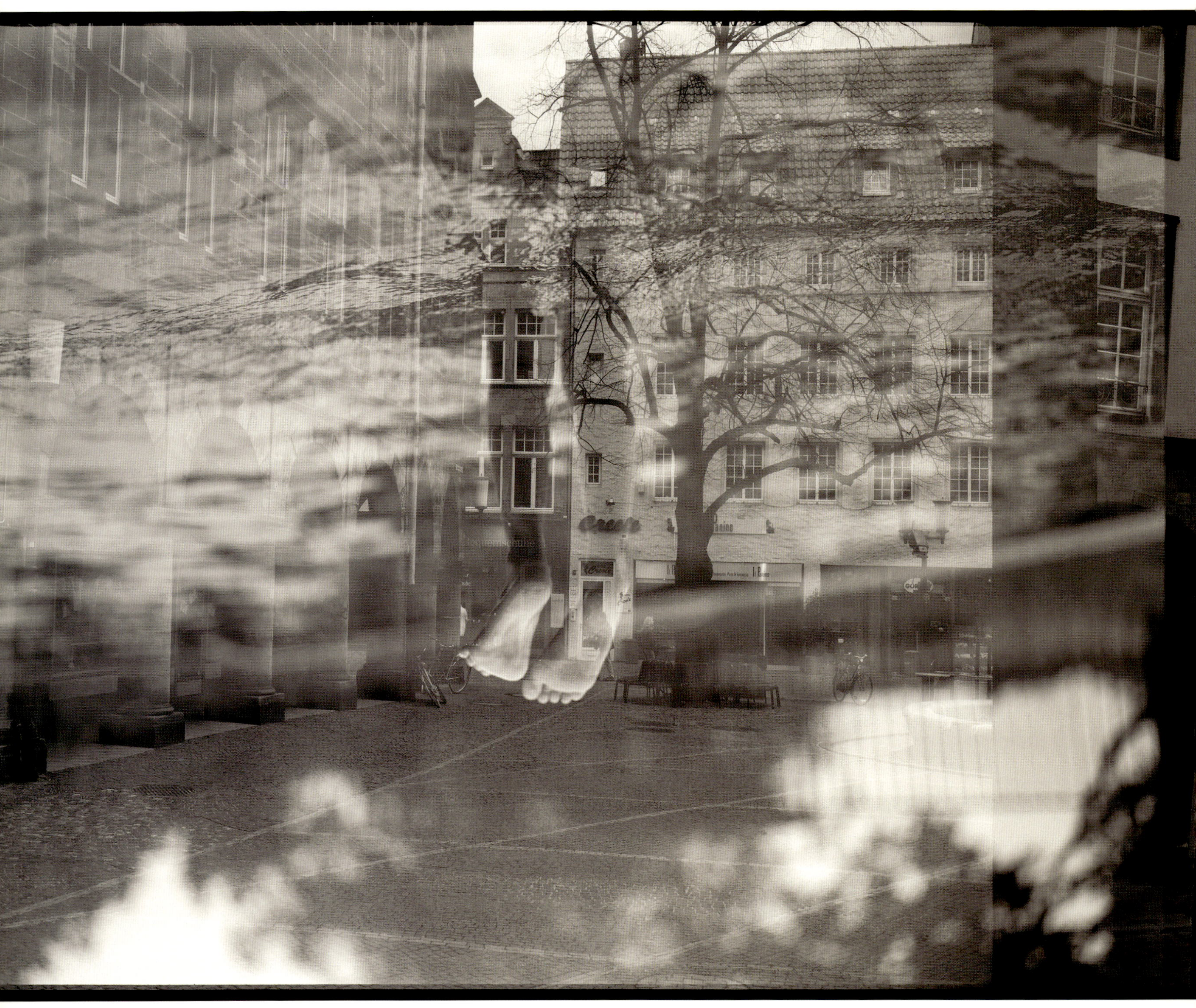

50   *swimmer plaza* (2002)

photography ('I can never deny that the thing has been there' [3]), what Rosalind Krauss refers to as:

the structural irony that would allow photography, this wrecker of unitary being, to perform that semiological sleight-of-hand whereby in the seamlessness of its physical surface the photograph seemed to summon forth the great guarantor of unity – raw nature, in all its presumed wholeness and continuity – to cover the tracks of photography's own citational operations. [4]

Awake/Asleep presents random and everyday landscapes and objects from Germany and Queensland, created from single rolls of film exposed first in one country, then packaged up by the photographer and mailed, to be exposed a second time after which they were processed and printed. In these converged images, both awake and asleep, we are dreaming, forgetting what we have seen while remaining captivated by the 'impossible exchange' between reality and image that speaks precisely to the dispersal of the subject in the time and silence of the photographic image. The photographic surface offers to transport us across the domain of an optic at once Romantic and modern, in the shift it engineers from the Romantic promise of proximity – the self's 'direct participation in natural processes and symbolic discourse about nature'[5], the lure of Caspar David Friedrich's cliff edge – to modernity's '[espousal of the] endless presence of the self'[6], whereby the world crowds back in on us through the frame and we recognize 'the multiple and mediated character of the objects' before us.[7]

At the same time, these double exposures return us to Etienne-Jules Marey's chronophotographs, articulating Henri Bergson's understanding of reality as itself movement.[8] For Bergson, as Marta Braun explains, 'the shapes of material objects are not properties of those objects but rather "snapshots taken by the mind of the continuity of becoming" '.[9] The division of the world into bodies and forms is finally transformed in Marey's pictures into the 'undivided fact' of time, the 'passage from rest to rest',[10] whereby the body itself is revealed as an animate and poetic machine, formed in and across the movement from one breath to the next. Marey's map of change thus complicates the unity of the image,[11] swamping its coherence with the dense tactility of light and energy. In this sense, the misted forms of *Light Matter* chart the blur of time as it passes 'from rest to rest' and

from body to body.

Walter Benjamin extends this understanding as the 'optical unconscious' of movement, the 'secret of 'what happens during the fraction of a second when a person steps out' that is revealed by '[p]hotography, with its devices of slow motion and enlargement'.[12] Through this micrological gaze, then, photography constitutes a Bergsonian 'empathy by which we place ourselves within the object',[13] with the photographic subject giving way to a dreaming self, both awake and asleep; to a lens recording only the effects of light and time.

The photographic double exposure takes up precisely this apophasis, attenuating the simultaneity of photographic signification in the light of its relation to accident, illusion and dream. In the sequential exposures of the film are captured reflections from two different times and places; in their superimposition is imagined a shared and simultaneous form. In this way, double exposure works to draw attention back to the mechanics of photography, the history of its machinery and the constant reinvention of its graphesis as the interplay between illusion and image.

The shared and unobtrusive actions of packaging up and posting photographic film across the globe sees the image skipping between formal divisions of night and day, blurring the light and the dark of two cameras and two continents. Derrida has of course shown us that such a transmission names the gap between sender and receiver, granting priority to neither; the 'Postal Principle' opens up not only the possibility of arrival but also of diversion and delay, so that communication and indeed representation itself are always in process. In this way, the postal principle 'regularly prevents [and] delays ... the depositing of [meaning]'.[14] Derrida notes that

to bind [signifier to signified] is immediately to supplement, to substitute, and therefore to represent, to replace… To bind therefore is also to detach, to detach a representative, to send it on a mission… A post effect. Of a postman charged with proceeding to a delivery. [15]

Awake/Asleep is structured thus around the aleatory possibilities of sending, receiving and losing, looking again at light and form as the stuff in between lenses and things.

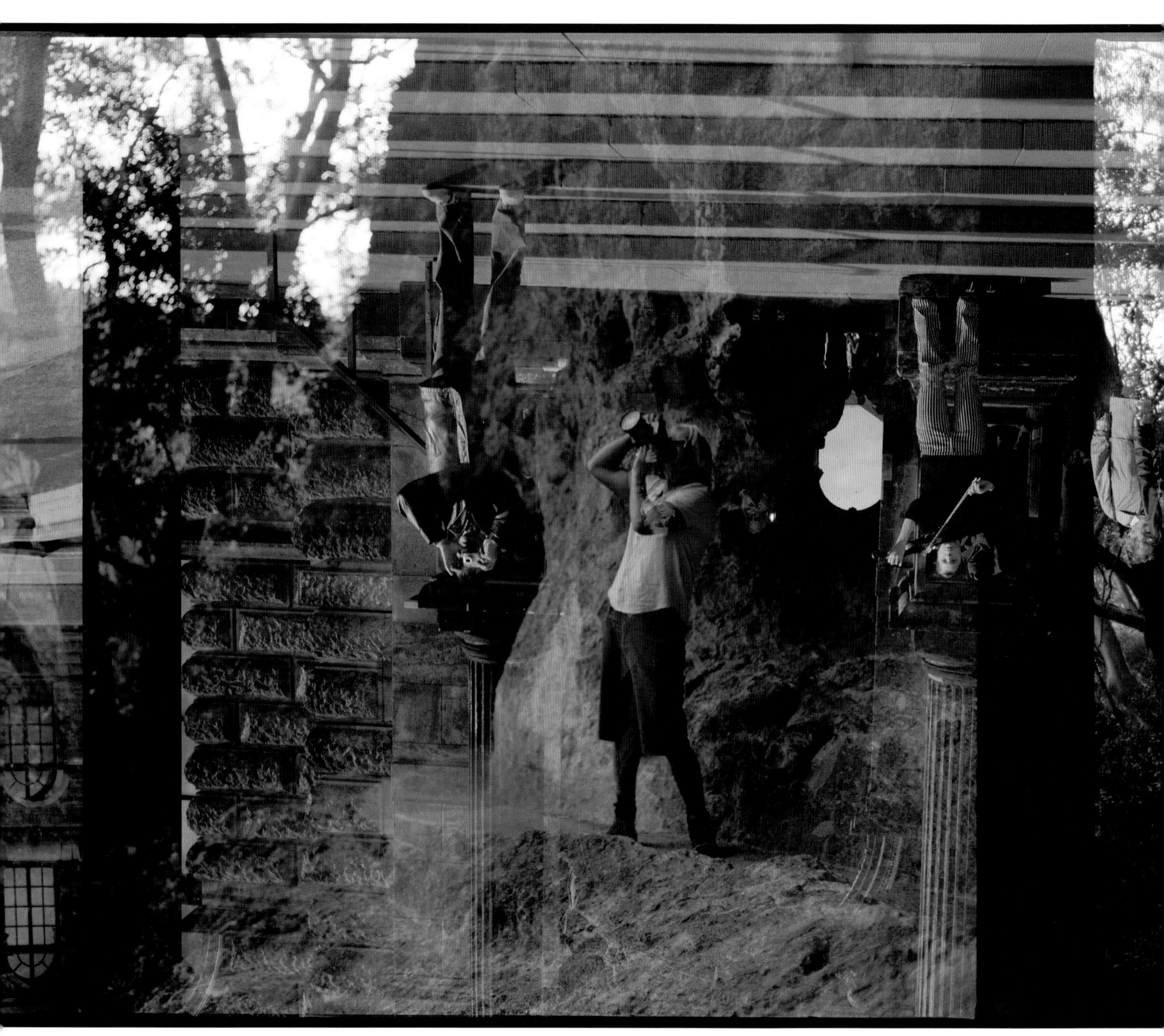

 photographer photographer (2005)

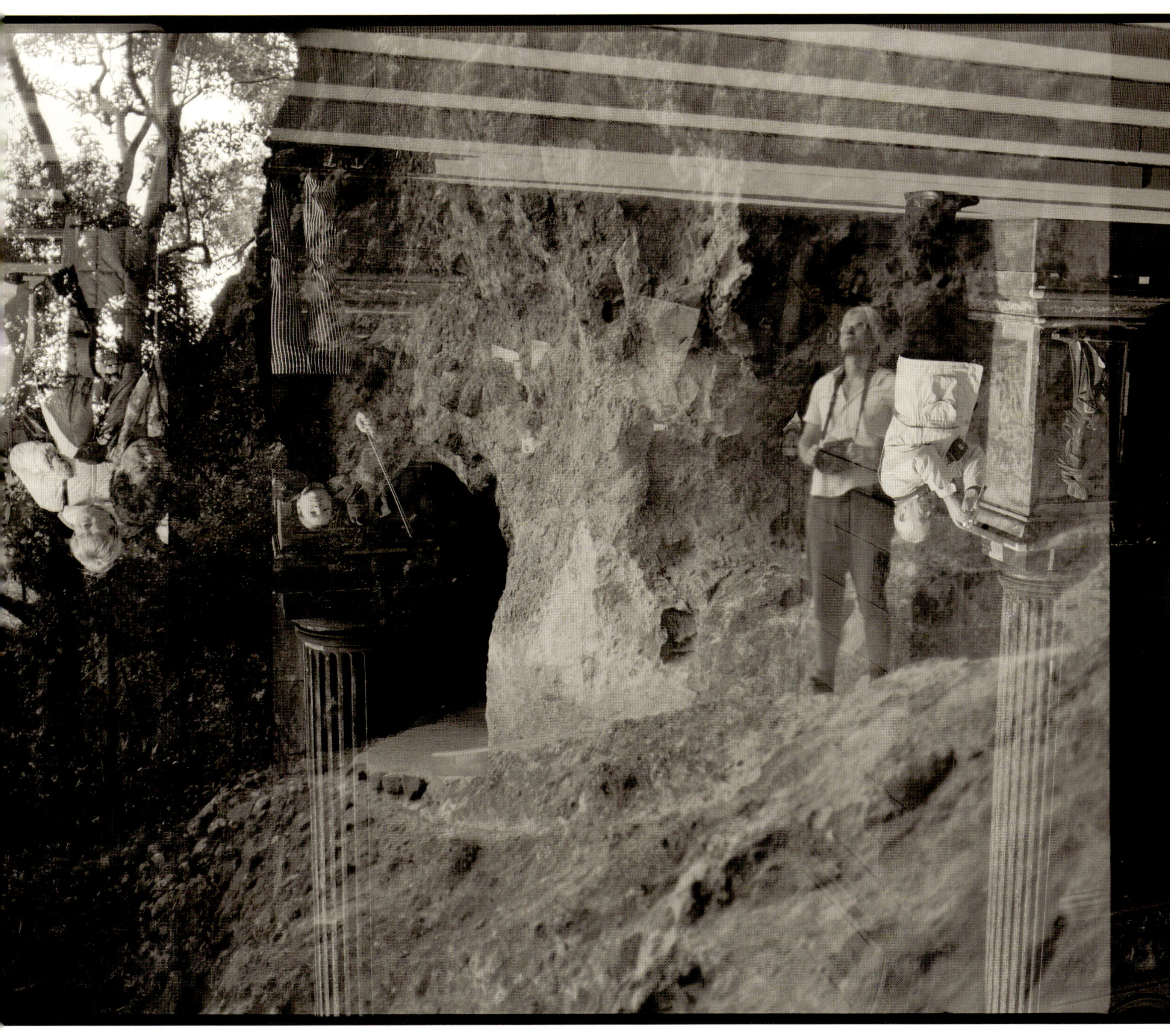

The viewer and the photographer are both doubled and literally displaced by this relay of exposure in the photographs; even though the places we see seem real, indeed familiar, enough, they do not fix any location for viewing. It is unclear how we are to look, whether from the north or the south, from up or from down, or suspended, flickering, somewhere between the two. The before and after, the here or the now of the finished image are likewise unclear; in place of such orientation's the viewer is drawn into a dispersed space of both looking and dreaming, the linguistic shifters themselves adrift. The process further materialises juxtapositions of natural and built environments, north/south oppositions and other antipodean tropes, rendering them tangible and in the process unhinging them somewhat from the coherence's of realism and reference. In this way, floodlit classical buildings are glimpsed through a suburban window frame; stone steps open into the bush; and an internal staircase looks in, Narnia-like, onto an obscured outdoors. The domestic materials of the house lurch into an open field, while the angular forms of a Hills Hoist or huge fronds of aloe or a horse underpin the base of a venerable castle.

In its constitution of the image, the perplexingly simple mechanism of photographic double exposure disperses light, rendering it no longer everywhere unremarkable; here light becomes the building block of castles literally in the air, the substance of vegetation superseding the cultural work of millennia. In a sense, then, the undoing of these naming binaries is a result of recording light, trapping it between two hemispheres, somewhere between night and day. Through double exposure these photographs fold the referent back on itself, leaving its claims to veracity and solidity strangely attenuated. Particular forms in the photographs take on an extreme irreality, losing all substance of their own, playing only with light and foregrounding the risks and contingencies of the photographic mechanism, so that clouds might look like a stain or smudge, branches could perhaps be just a scratch on the film. The close-up layering of snowy earth seems simply magical, the faint fronds of trees imprinting another level of texture into the surface of the snow, while rocks divide, Escher-like, to reveal the entrance to a cave full of pure light, open to another sky that recalls to us once more the Romantic promise of Nature's closeness.

Awake/Asleep offers the experience of flux outside or beyond narrative, swooping across the globe, a journey through the night to another night, at the ends of the earth. The time of this passage is fixed not by narrative structure but by the photographic image with its lucid simultaneity. Seasonal and diurnal relations are compressed into the stillness of a single image, which takes on the fullness of a day and a night, of the incidental spaces of the northern and southern divisions of the earth. In this way, the photographs invest the banality of an antipodean reverse with the mechanics of concurrence. The photograph becomes the locus of the compression of time into an image, which is an illusion, a locus where forms collide, where the properties of materials and states of matter shift unreliably, and where objects are pushed into an impossible proximity. Europe is at once dwarfed by tropical foliage, and insistent in its perennial forms – crenellations, flagstones, cobbles. A fairytale history is at play here, a displaced familiarity of forms and materials coming to us all at once with traceries of wintry branches over tropical city scapes; a Brisbane street lurching sharply upwards into an inverted castle.

Textures dominate the photographs, interanimating distinct worlds where forms meet and collide: leaves superimposed on cobblestones look for an instant like ripples on water; darker shapes lose their density so that a fir tree takes on the large pale forms of water lilies; the ripples on a pond flow through the flagstones, the denseness of stone no longer sustainable. In this way, nature is seen to be already marked by form, already abstract and so, through the relay of transmission, the passage of the film across the earth, a teleology of loss is bypassed through the temporality of the image.

For Benjamin, photography allows us to discover

[the] physiognomic aspects of visual worlds which dwell in the smallest things, meaningful yet covert enough to find a hiding place in waking dreams but which, enlarged and capable of formulation, make the difference between technology and magic visible.[16]

So too in *Awake/Asleep*, through the mechanism of the camera, distance is flattened into close-up, and reverie is drawn back into introspection. Dense with the textures of their own figuration, the histories and futures of images, the differences of scale and orientation and the forms and times of growth, the photographs tease us with time;

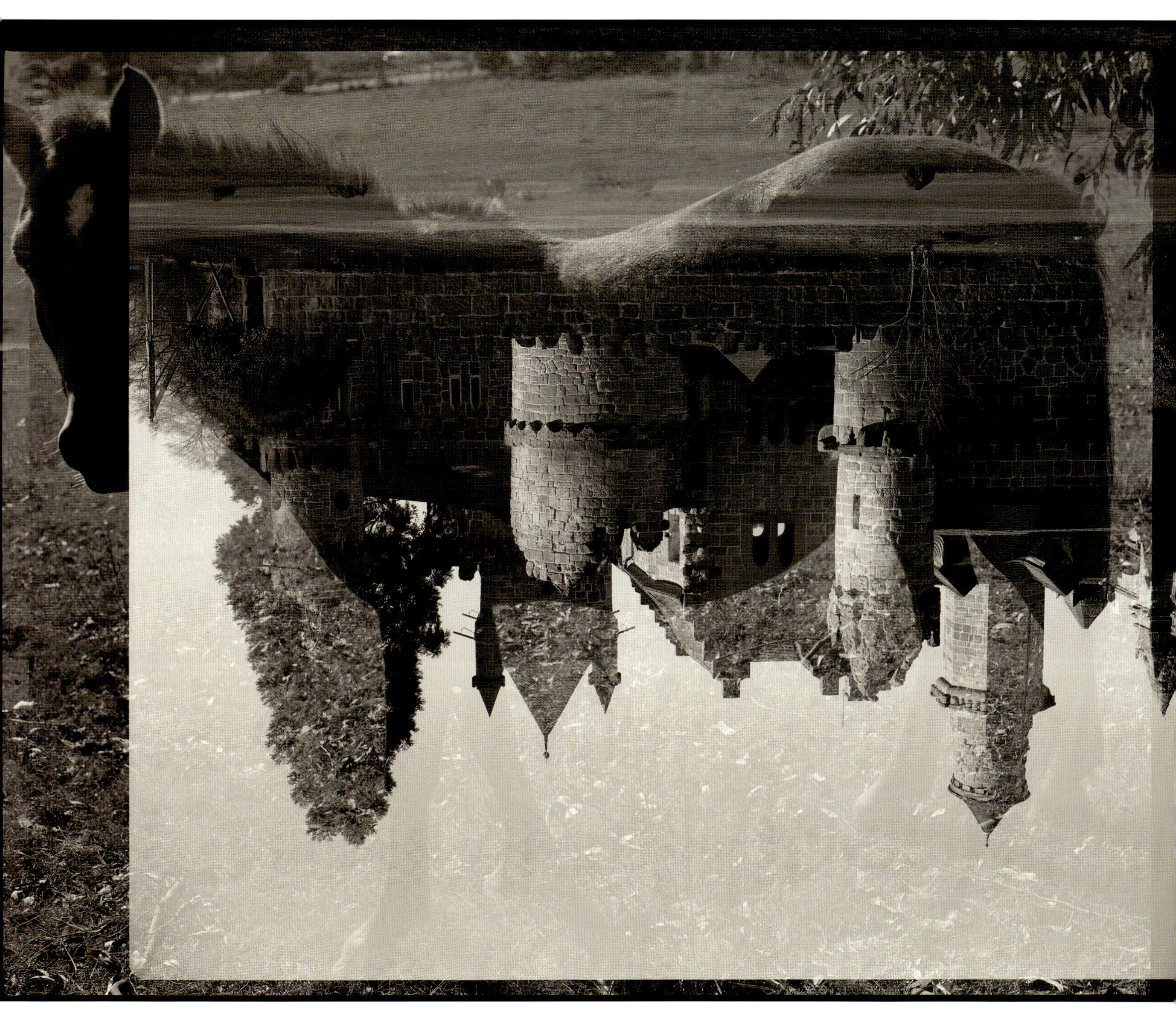

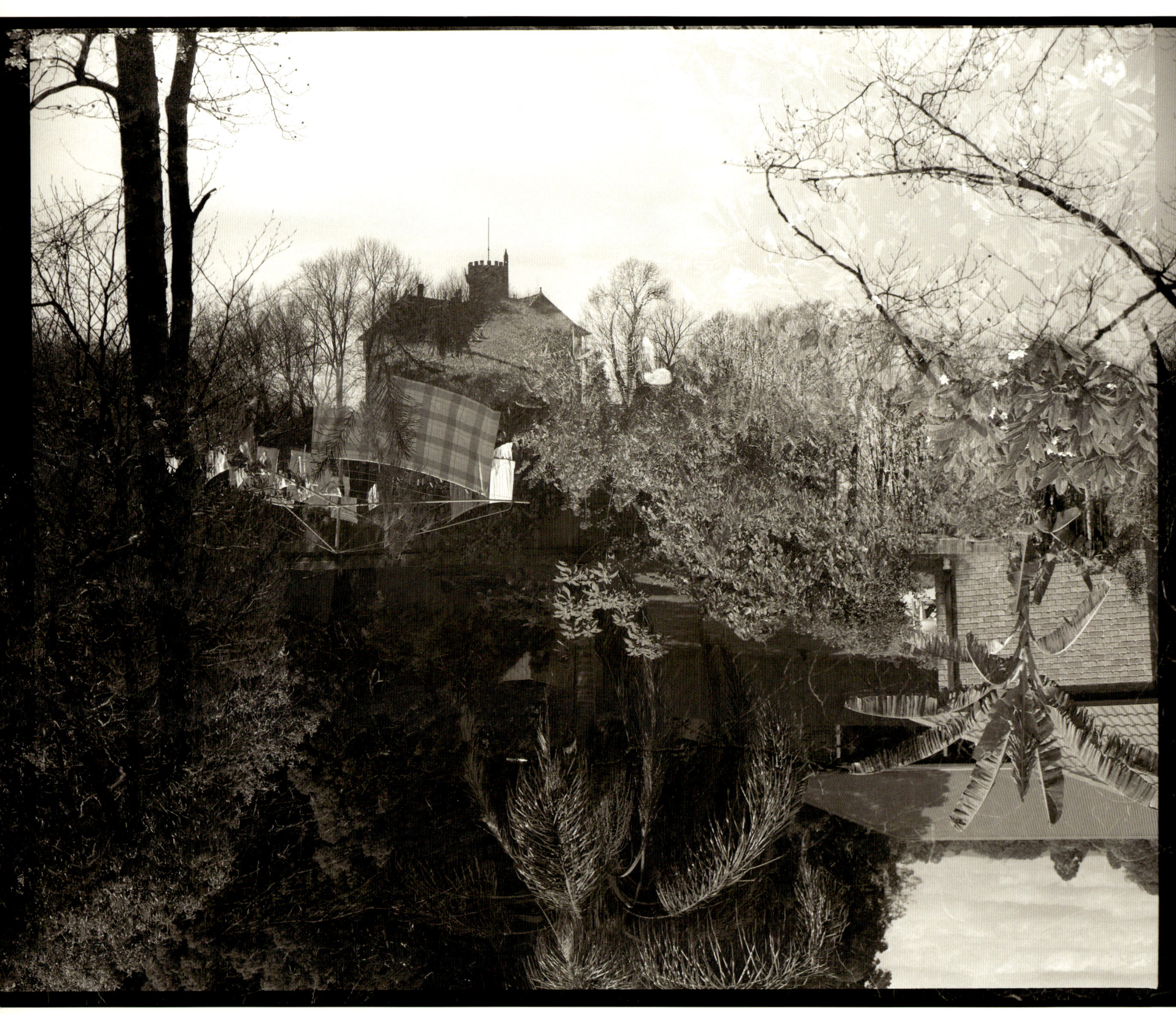

56   *backyard schloss* (2004)

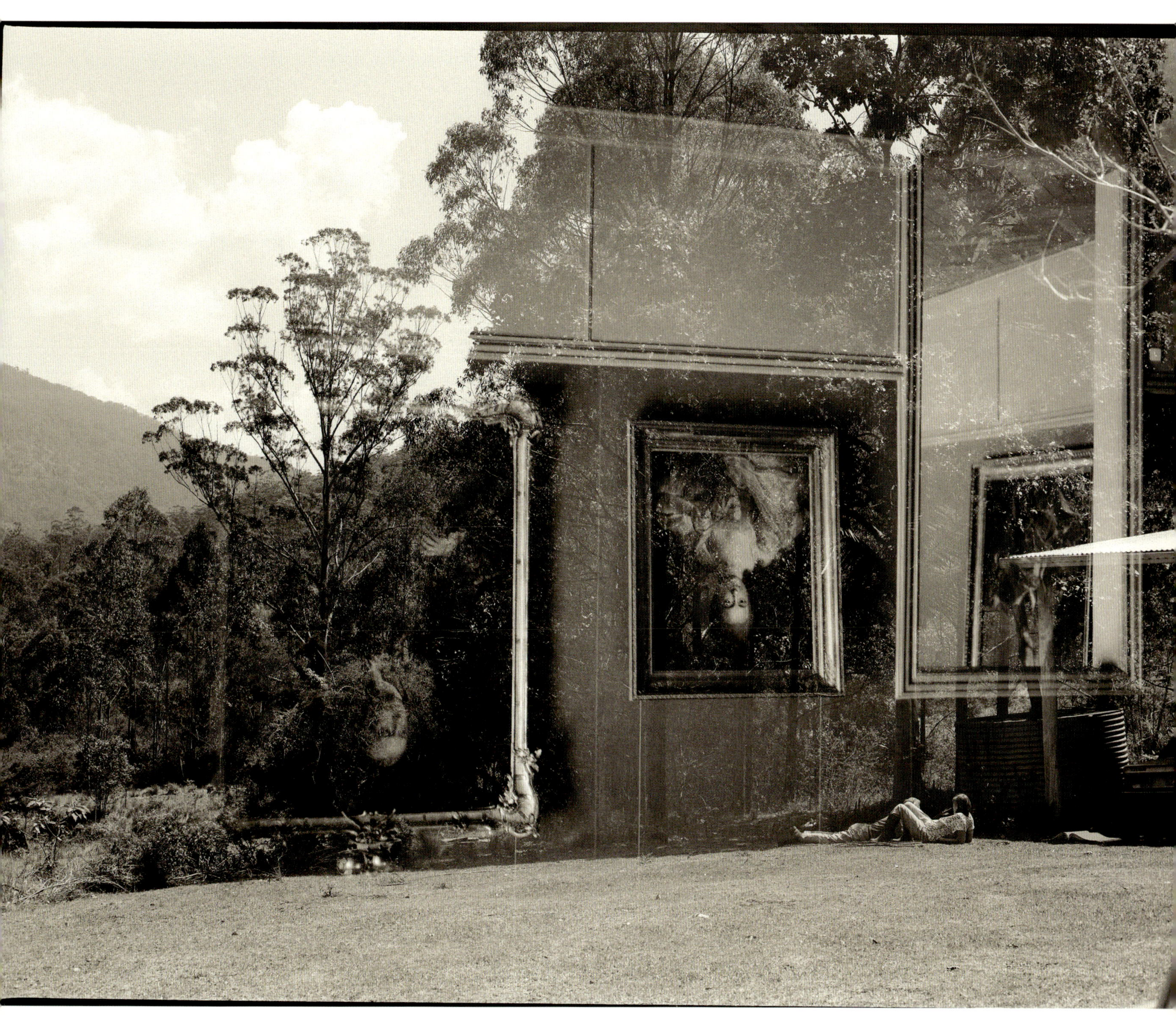

rather than resting alone with our dreams, they find us awake / asleep.

Dr Brigitta Olubas
University of New South Wales

Footnotes

[1] Rexer: 128

[2] Baudrillard

[3] Barthes: 76

[4] Krauss: 290

[5] Rexer: 131

[6] Bolter and Grusin: 353

[7] Bolter and Grusin: 353

[8] Henri Bergson, *Matter and Memory*, quoted in Braun: 278

[9] Henri Bergon, *Creative Evolution*, quoted in Braun: 278-279

[10] Henri Bergson, *Matter and Memory*, quoted in Braun 278

[11] see Braun: 66: 'Since the advent of linear perspective in the Renaissance, the frame of an image has, with rare exceptions, been understood to enclose a temporal and spatial unity. We read what occurs within the frame as happening at a single instant in time and in a single space.'

[12] Benjamin: 243

[13] Braun: 277

[14] Derrida: 54

[15] Derrida: 394

[16] Benjamin: 243-244

References

Roland Barthes, *Camera Lucida*, Fontana, London, 1984

Jean Baudrillard, 'Photography, Or the Writing of Light' Ctheory 2000 http://www.egs.edu/faculty/baudrillard/baudrillard-photography-or-the-writing-of-light.html viewed on 24.04.06

Walter Benjamin, 'A Small History of Photography', in *One Way Street* (trans Edmund Jephcott and Kingsley Shorter) London and New York: Verso, 2000

Henri Bergson, *Matter and Memory*

Henri Bergson, *Creative Evolution*

Jay David Bolter and Richard Grusin, 'Remediation', *Configurations* 4.3 (1996): 311-358.

Marta Braun, *Picturing Time: the work of Etienne-Jules Marey* (1830-1904), Chicago: University of Chicago Press, 1992.

Jacques Derrida, *The Post Card: from Socrates to Freud and Beyond* (trans. Alan Bass), Chicago: University of Chicago Press, 1987.

Rosalind E. Krauss, 'Reinventing the Medium: Art and Photography', *Critical Inquiry* 25.2 (Winter 1999): 289-305

Lyle Rexer, *Photography's Antiquarian Avant-Garde: The New Wave in Old Processes*, New York: Harry N. Abrams, 2002.

 overleaf: *beach monument* (2005)

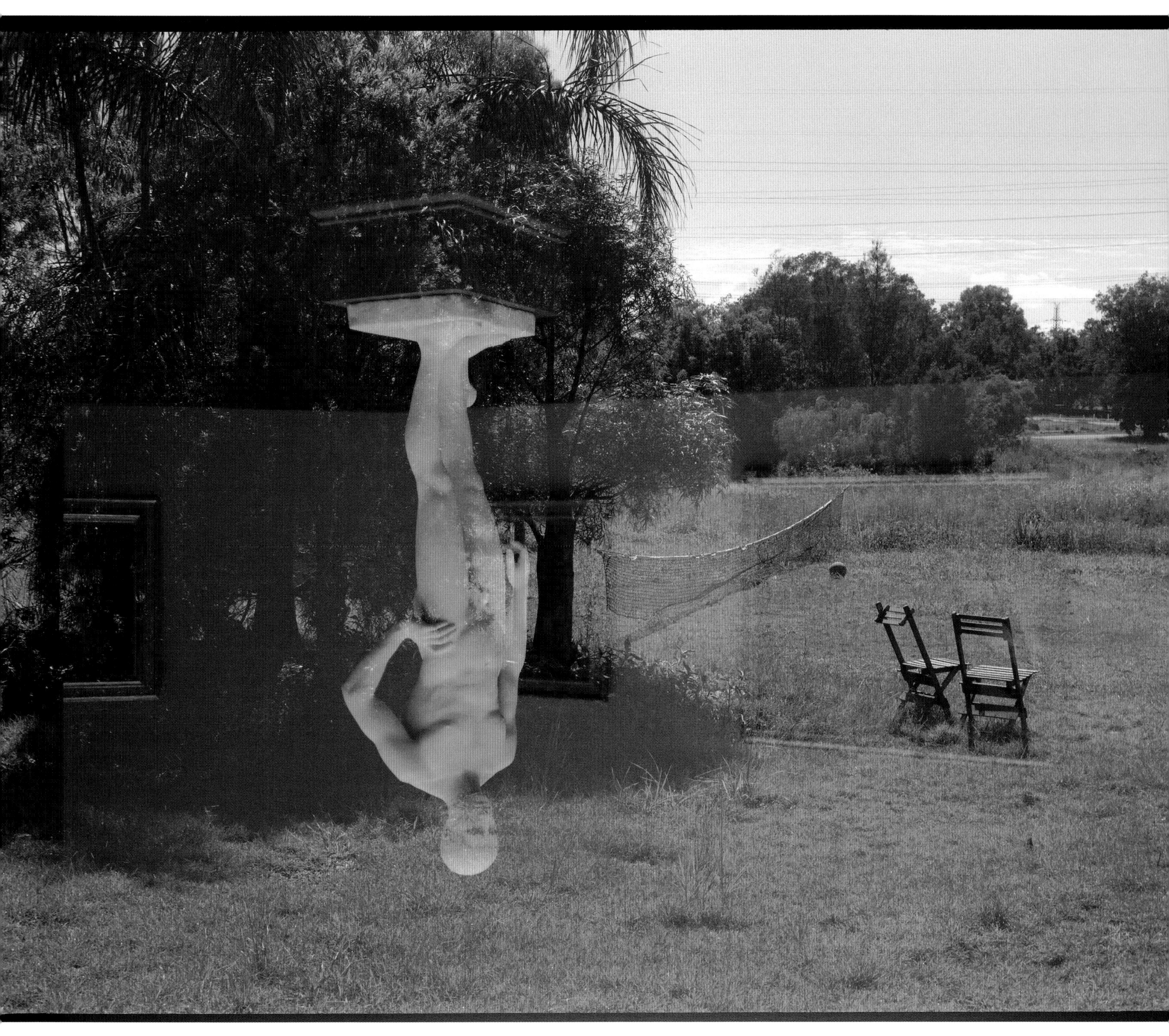

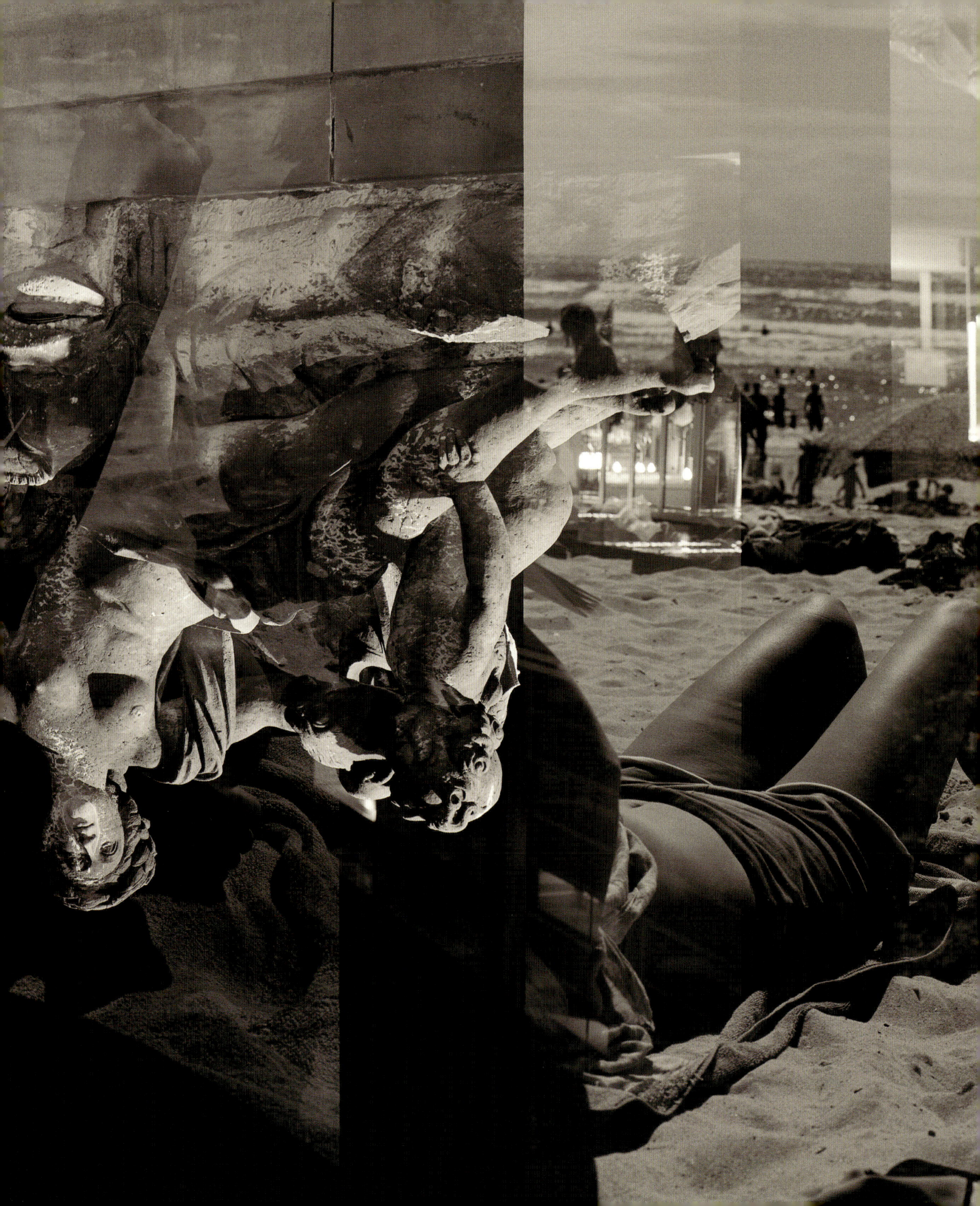

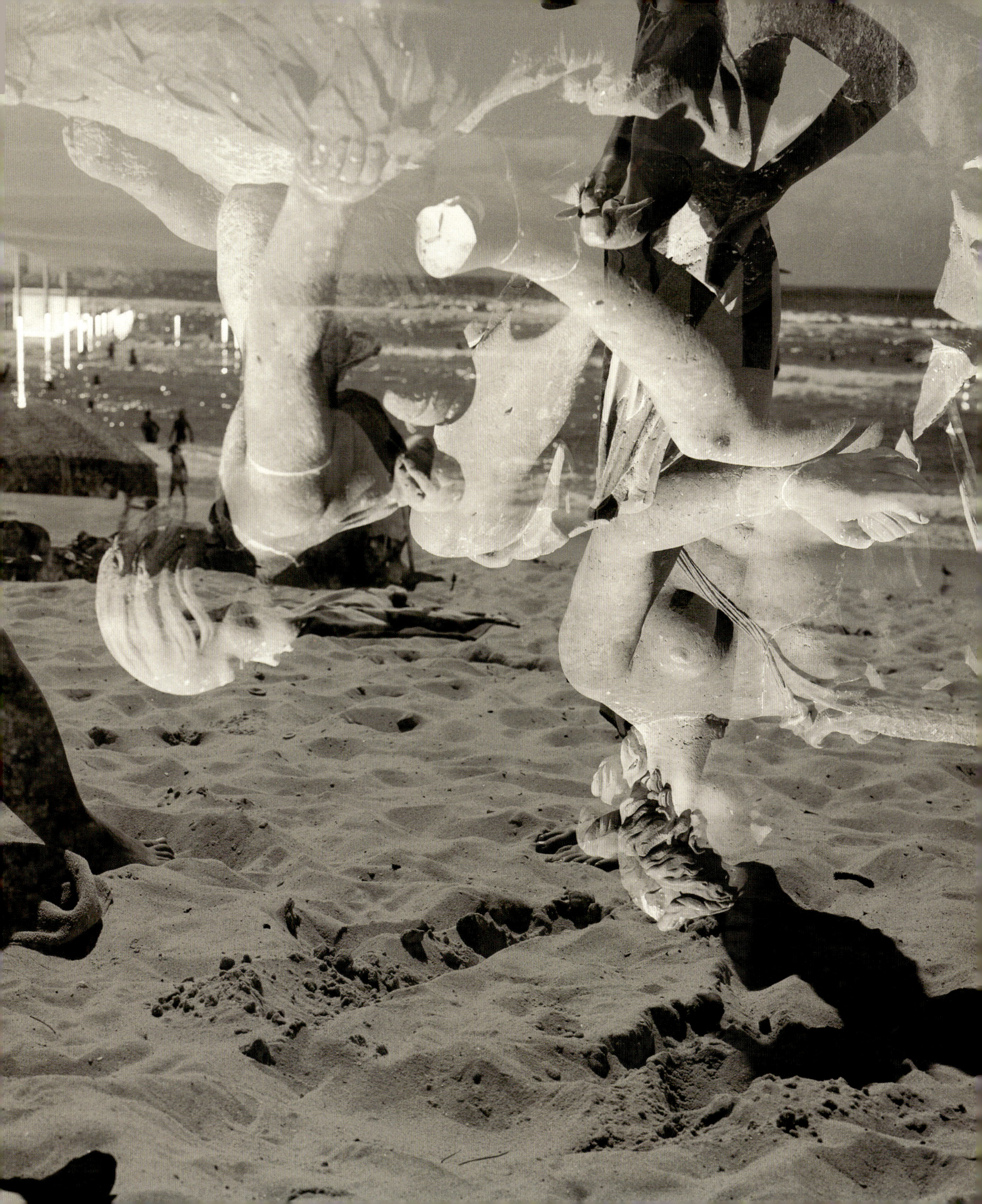

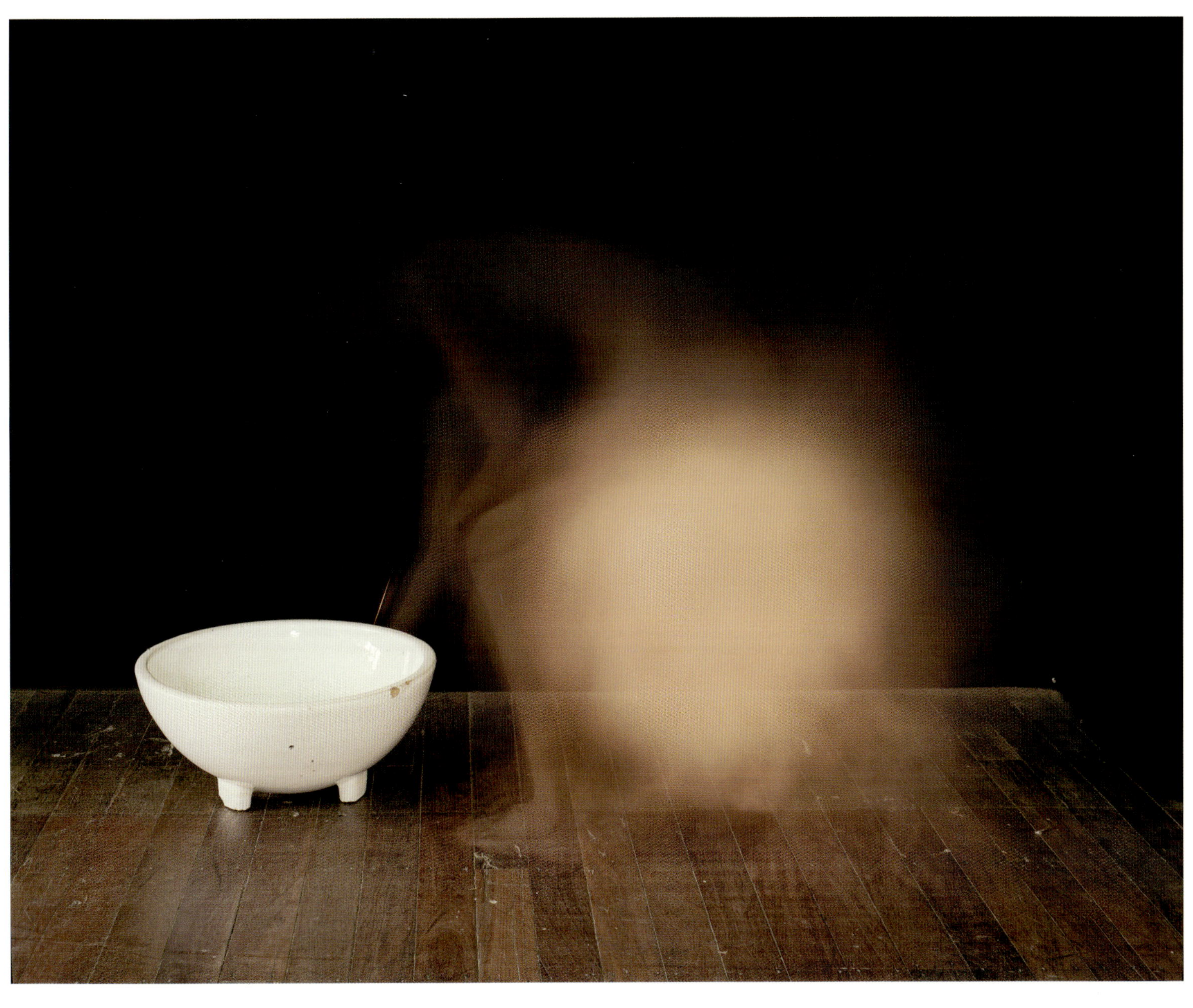

Shadow Matter (1999)

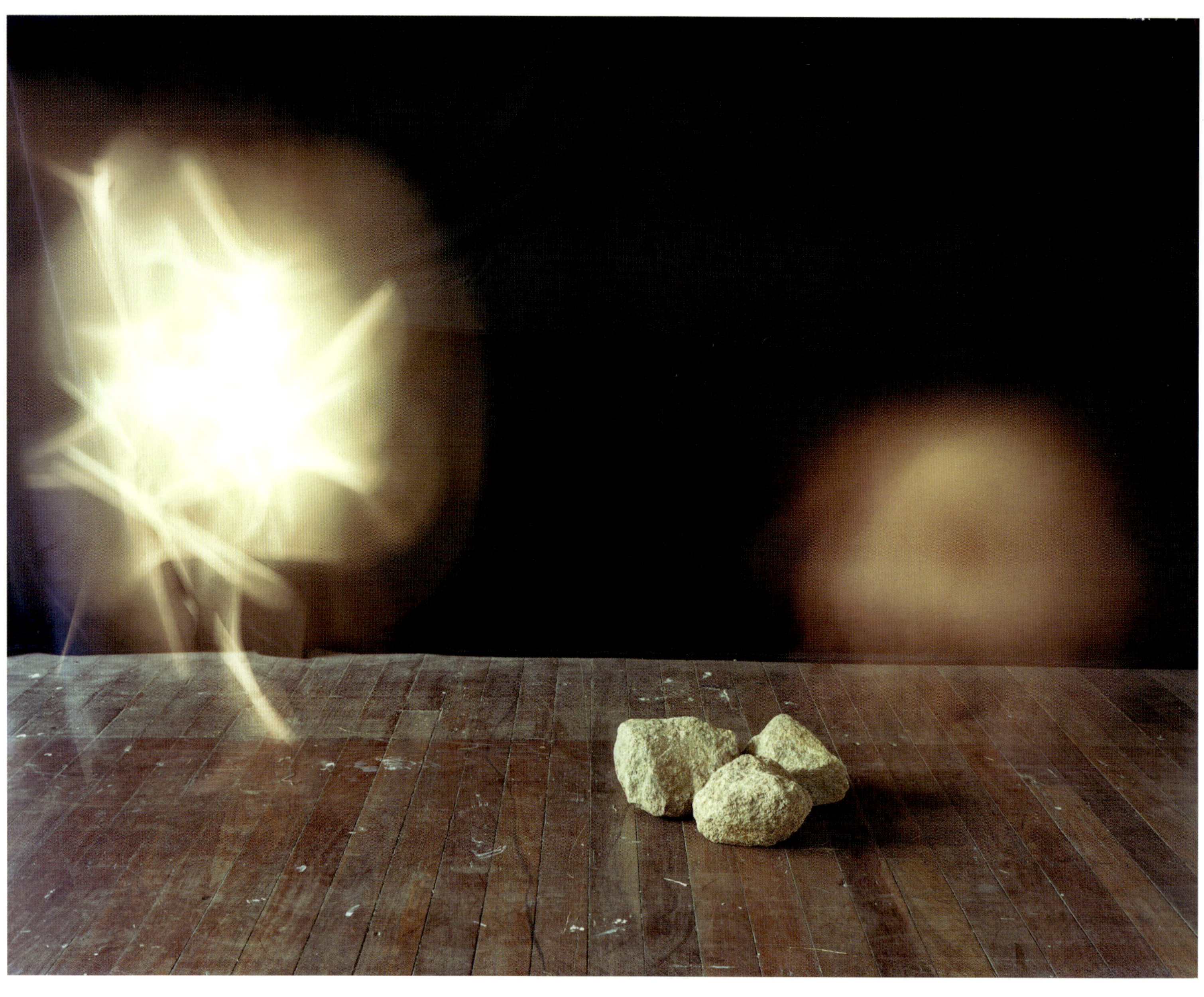

64   *Three light forms* (1999)

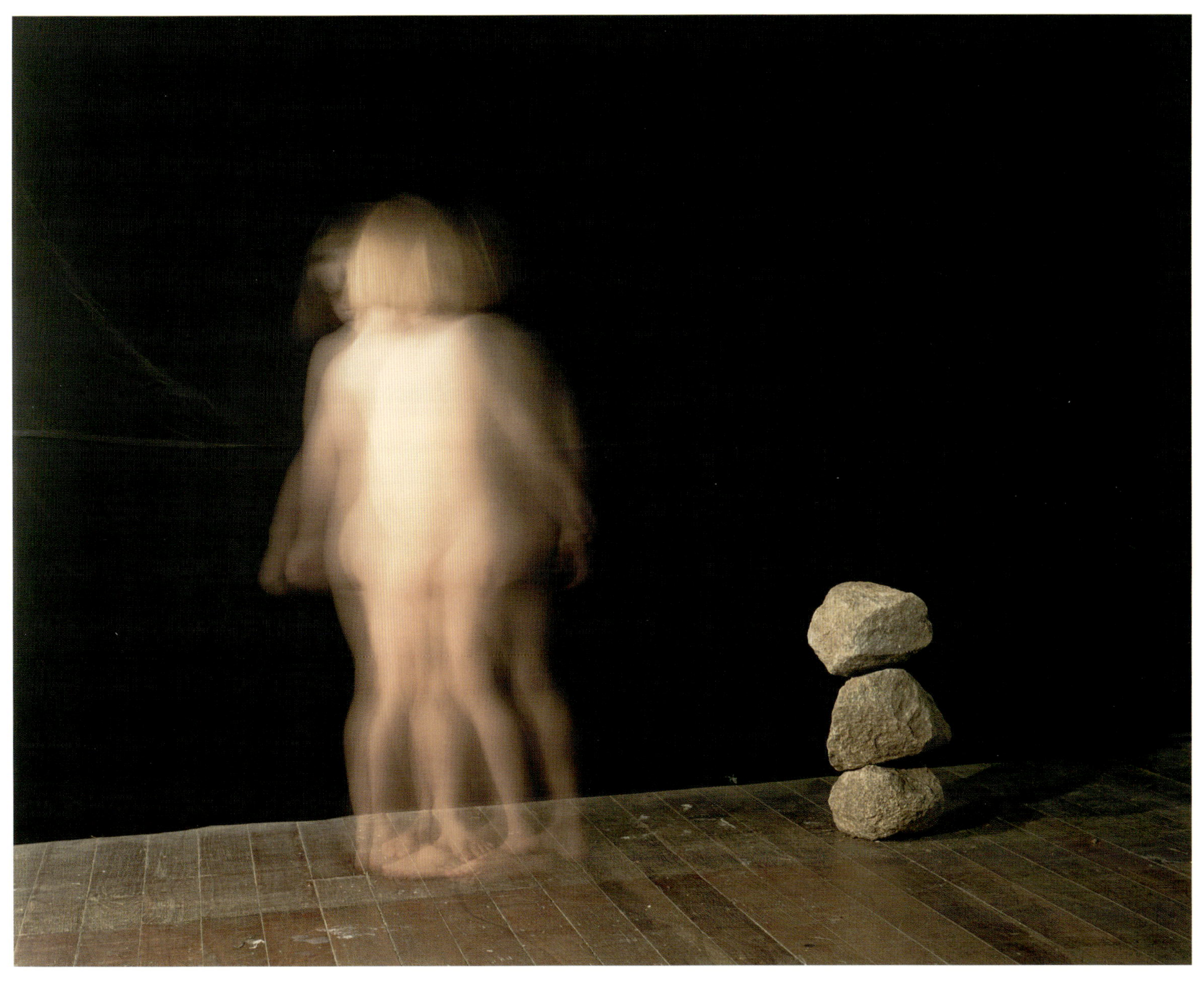

Three graces (1999)   65

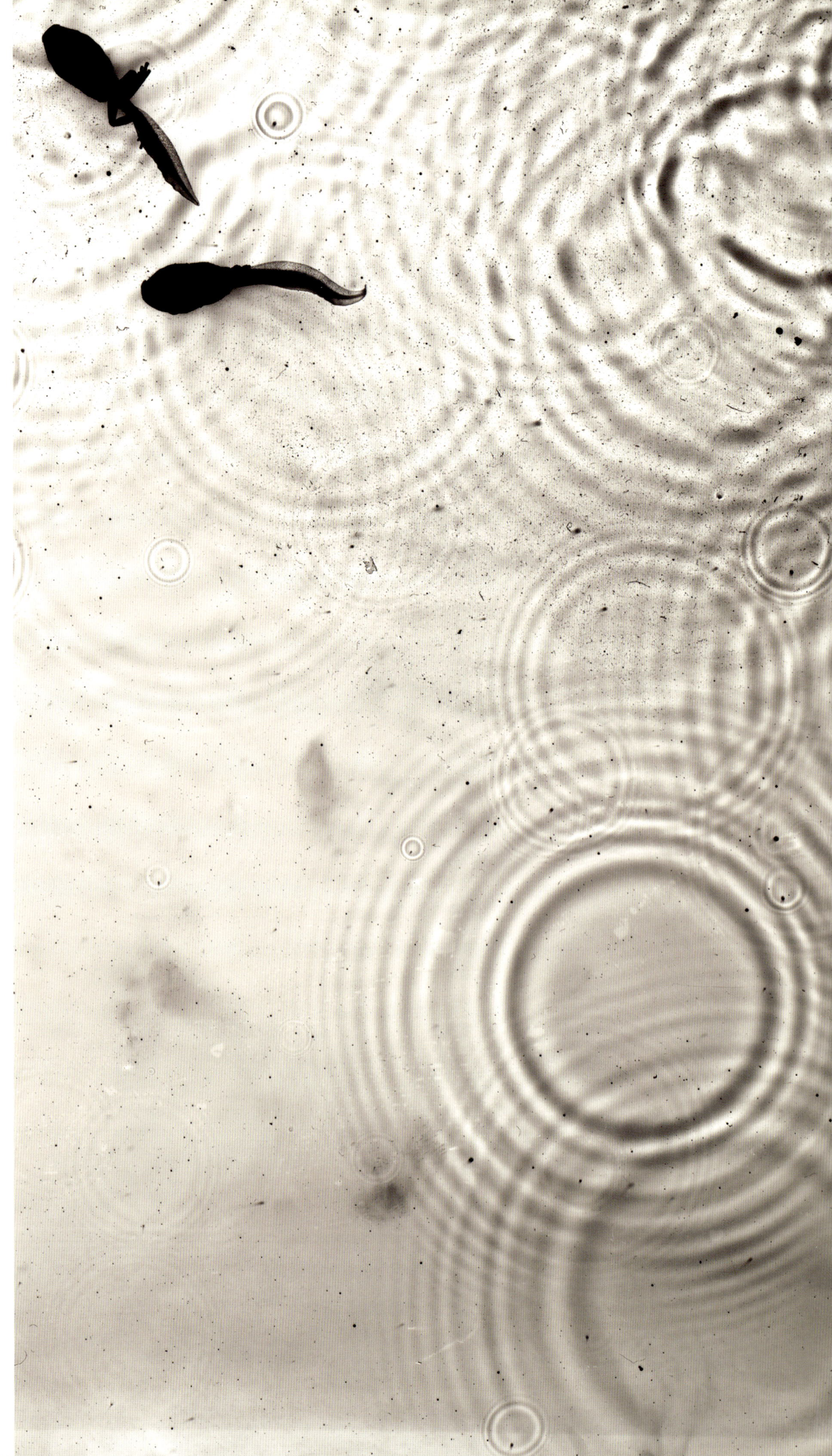

Untitled (2004-2006)

overleaf:
Wait a whiles (2004-2006)

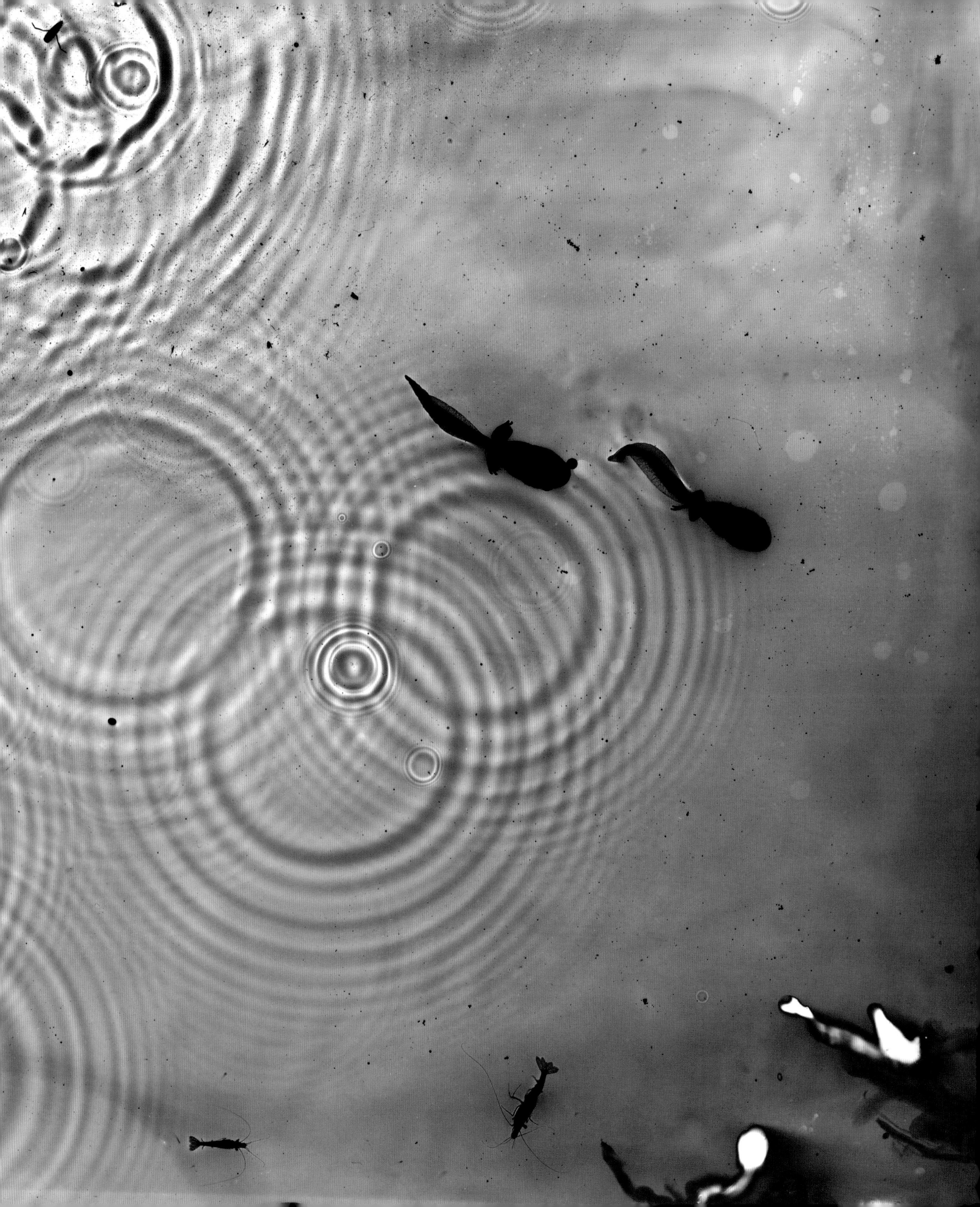

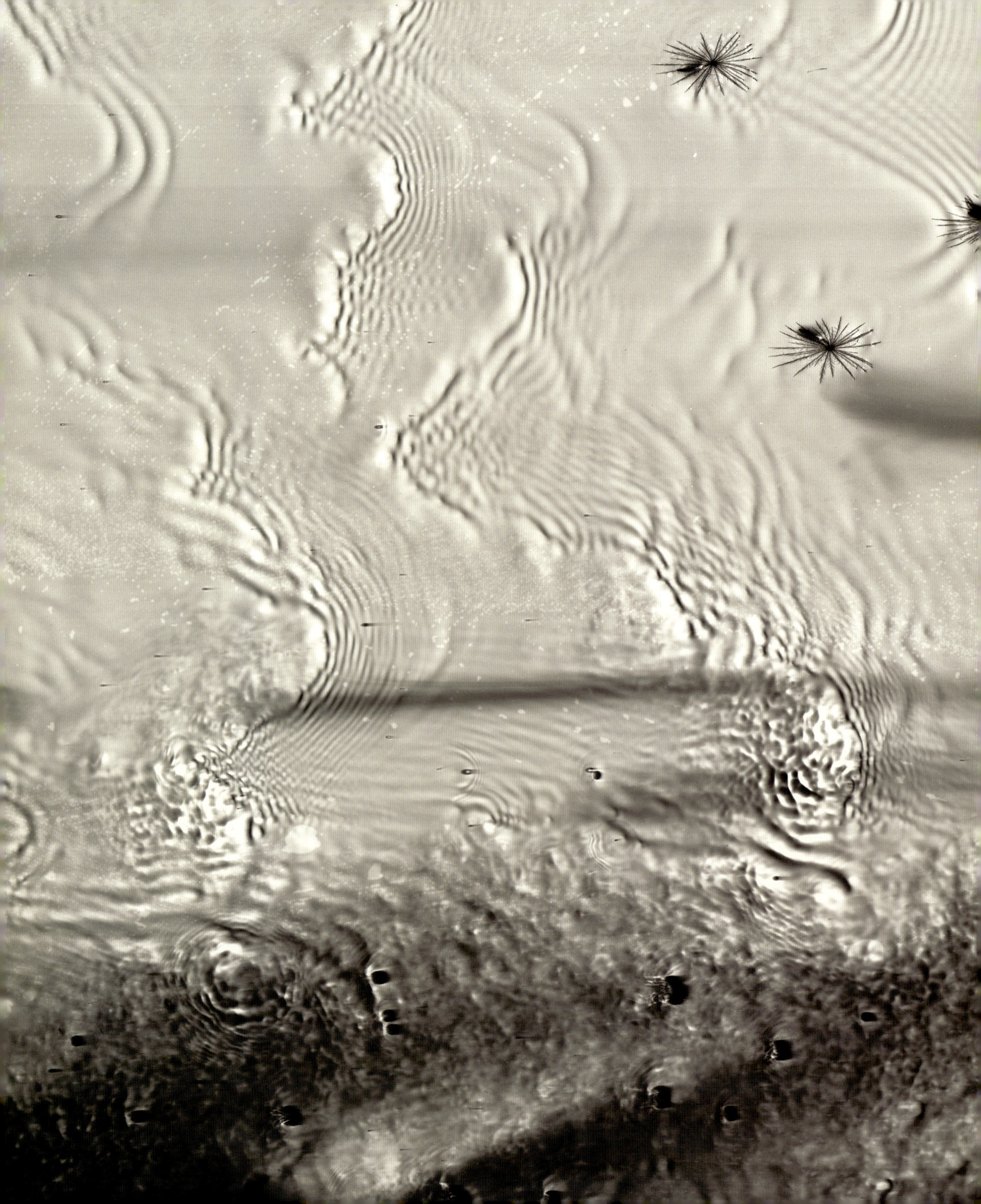

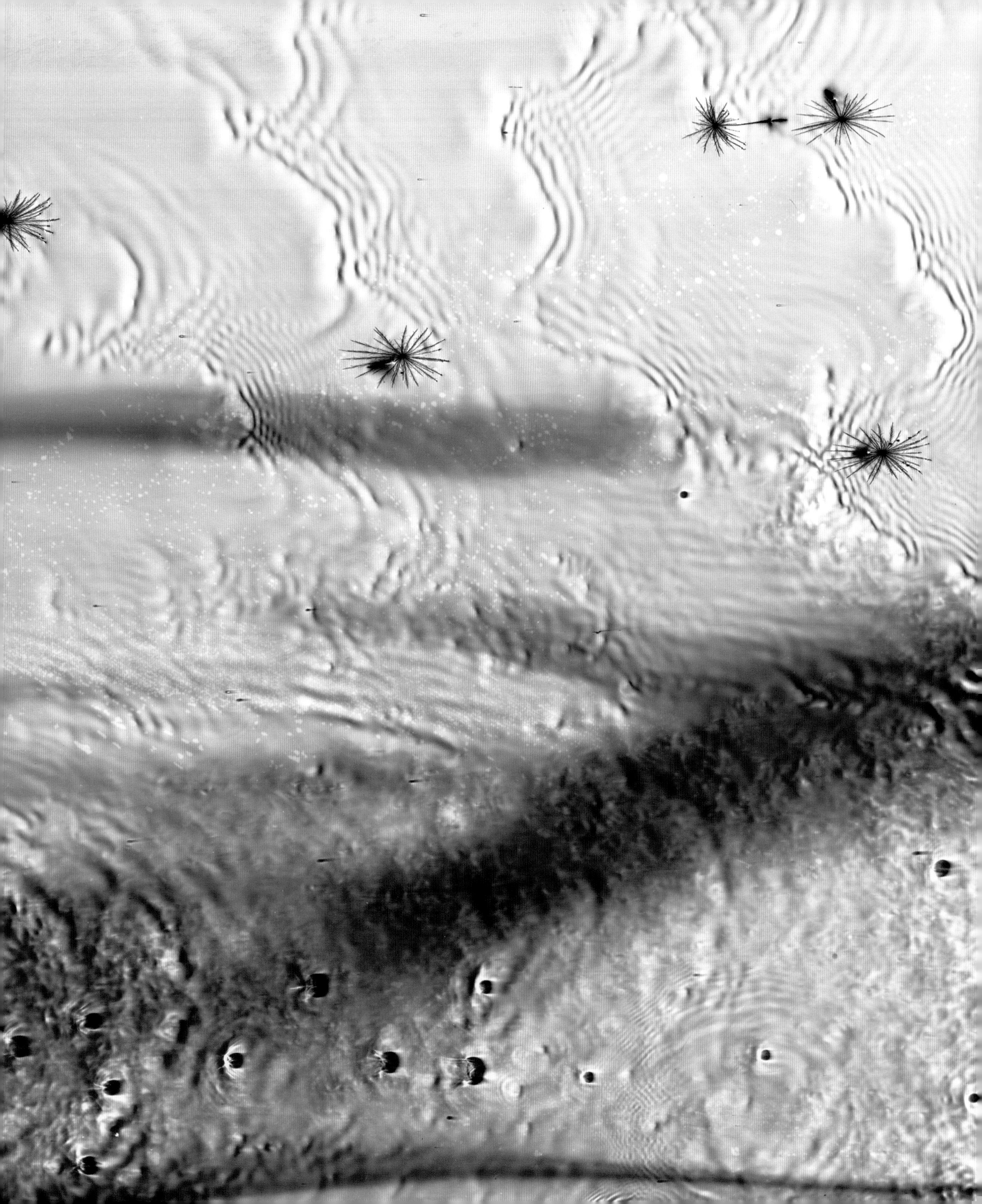

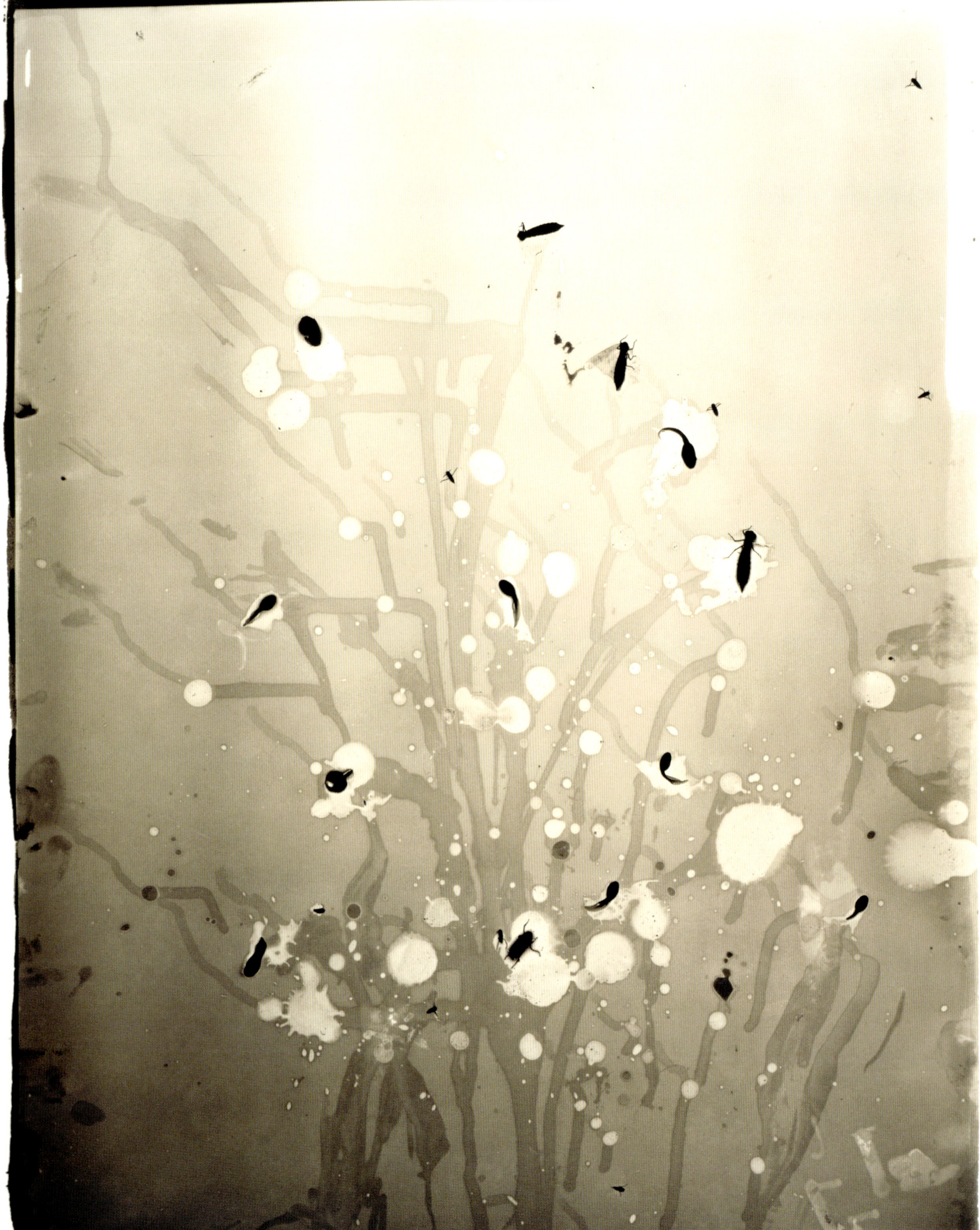

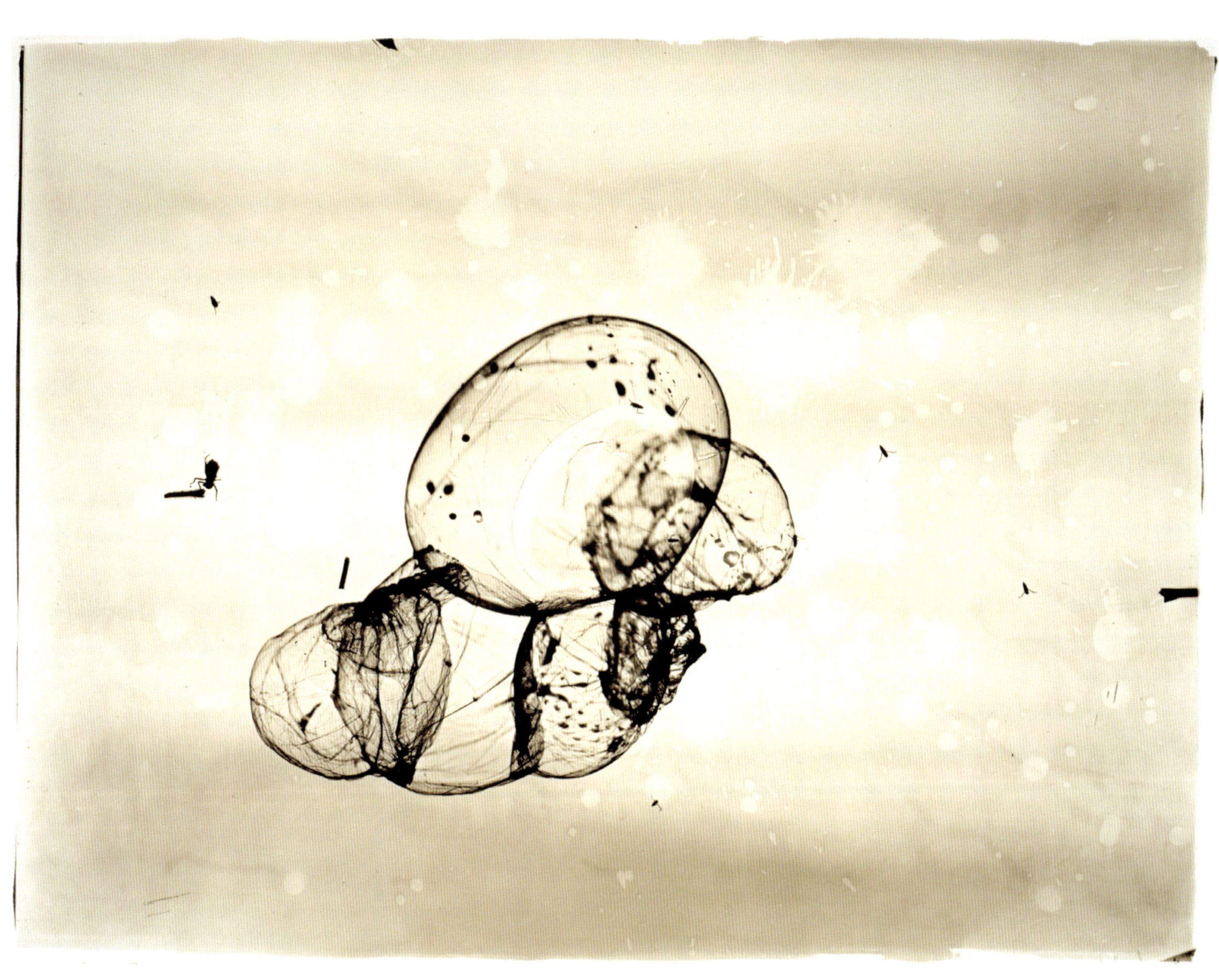

opposite: *Tree of life* (2001)
above: *Untitled* (2001)

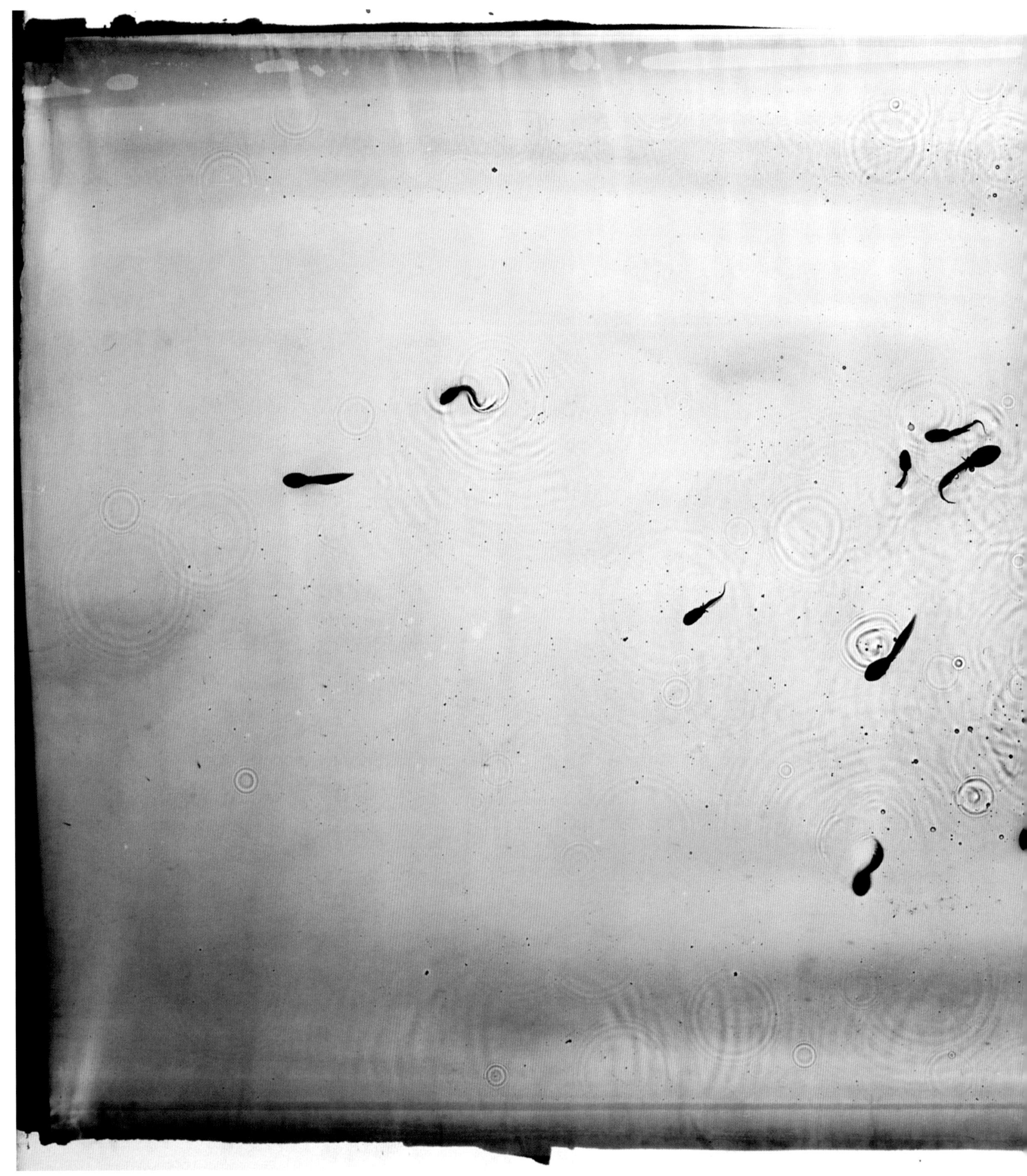

   After heavy rain (2001)

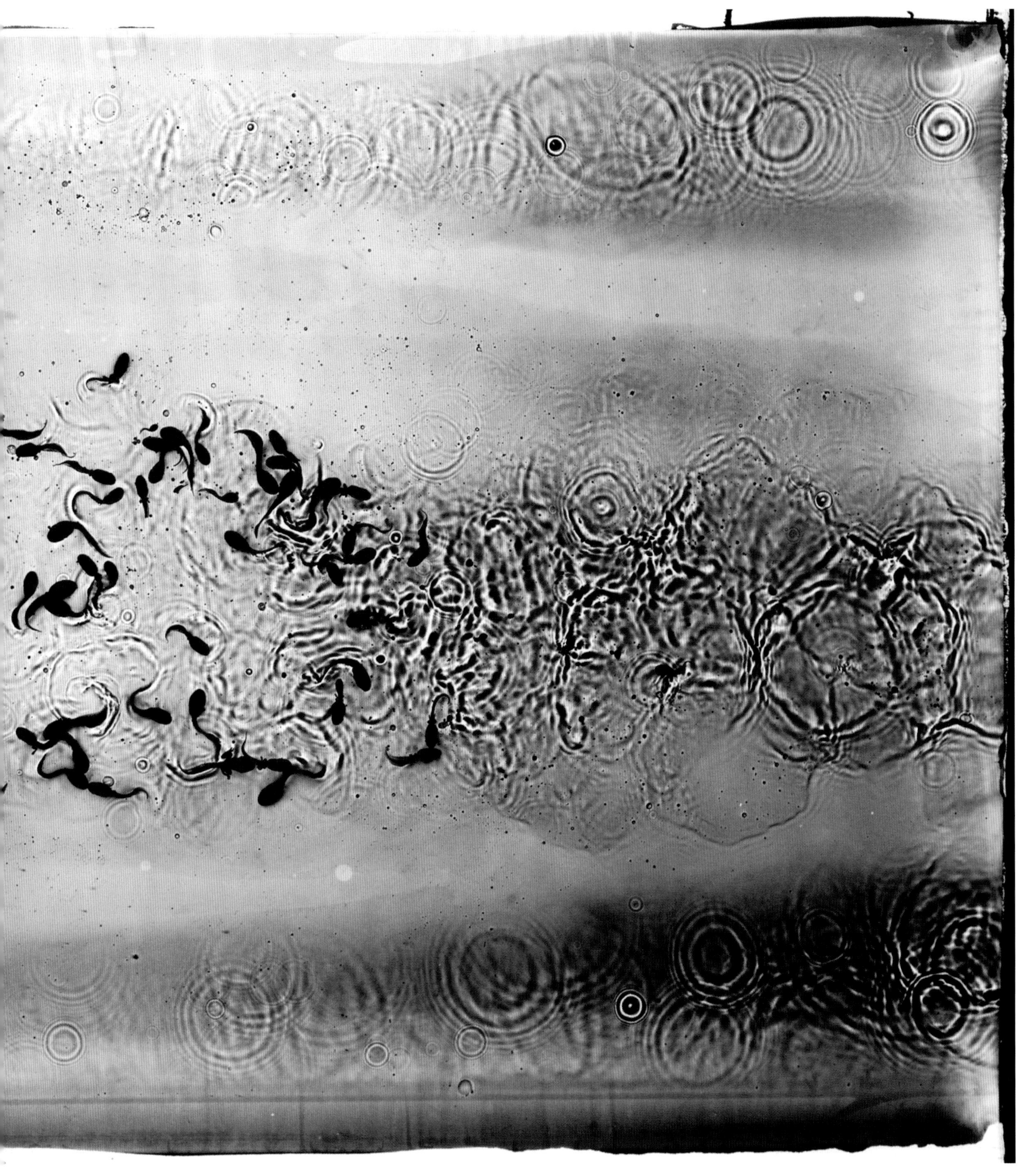

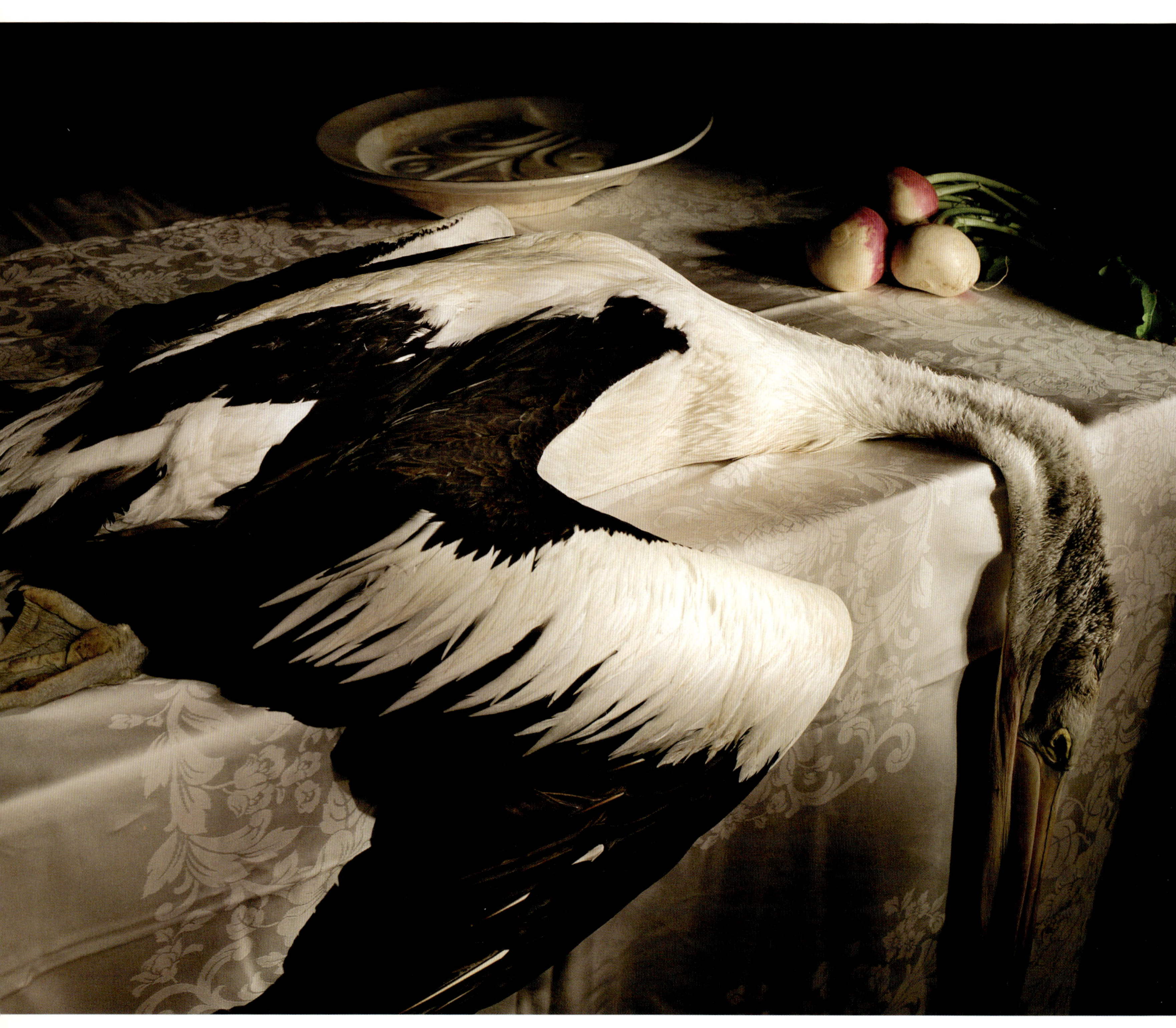

    Pelican with turnips (1992)

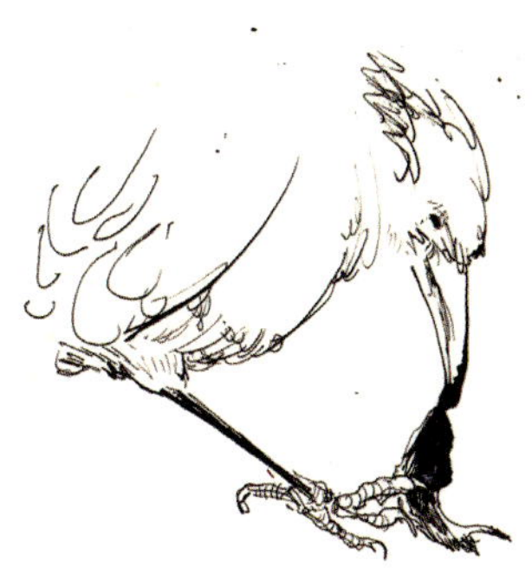

Marian Drew: Australiana/Still Life

Laid across tables as if for a feast, the creatures that populate Marian Drew's recent body of photographs are repellent in their limpness, and quietly shocking in their rupturing of domestic order. The excessive fussiness of starched, embroidered linen and patterned china is heightened by these carcasses, which retain a certain brutality no matter how elegantly they might be arranged. The air of anticipation and optimism that accompanies a splendidly laden table is infused here with the unmistakable stench of death. Drew's prints however, with their seductively rich colours, pleasing compositions and sensuous textures, harmonise these violent contrasts into seamless images, sidestepping sensationalism in conveying the horror of their subject matter. Instead it seeps out slowly, like blood.

For the animals and birds in Drew's photographs are all Australian natives: pelicans, fruit bats, magpies, rosellas, bandicoots, wombats, galahs and kangaroos. Each has met its demise through the encroachment of humans into its habitat – hit by a car, killed by a domestic pet, or stunned by power lines. They are part of the residue of environmental degradation, littering roadsides and washed up on beaches: the collateral of the clash between nature and culture. Since European settlement, Australia has had one of the highest rates of species extinction in the world, its unique and fragile ecosystems eroded or destroyed through land clearing, industry, urban development and the introduction of alien predators. Road kill is widely accepted as part of the landscape, with wandering animals considered an occupational hazard on rural highways, necessitating roo bars and insurance policy clauses.

Titling the series *Australiana*, Drew places this material evidence right before our eyes, into the heart of what is held dear and true: the home. It is presented in the form of still life, the artistic genre that has represented the domestic space for centuries, reflecting abundance and refinement back to ourselves like a mirror. These creatures are not viewed from behind car windows or hanging from lines high above; they are there on the kitchen table, amongst the props that confirm to us that we are a breed apart from beasts. Their presence disturbs this comfort, implicating our involvement in the carnage, whether knowingly or not. For it is precisely the maintenance of this veneer of civilisation, in this ancient and inscrutable place, that has resulted in the dreadful body count that shows no evidence of abating, with little effort undertaken to determine its full scope.

While appearing as perhaps the most direct of Drew's works in terms of its processes and the urgency of its subject matter, the *Australiana* series continues the artist's exploration into the possibilities of photographic truth. The photograph, as a document of an event or moment, retains a relationship to real, lived experience, no matter how much it is manipulated. Its ability to cohere disparate elements into a single image has been a key aspect of Drew's photographic work over the past two decades, which incorporates elements of painting, drawing, performance, installation, sculpture and projection in richly layered images that maintain a sense of process and the unfolding of time. With their blurred bodies, lines drawn in light and ghostly traces of figures come and gone, Drew's earlier photographs capture the transformation of objects, bodies and materials as they move between states. Although definitively still, the *Australiana* works nevertheless retains a sense of temporality, as their elaborate constructions, set up for the camera, record the passing of tiny lives.

Drew's images have an obvious referent in European still-life painting, which flourished throughout the continent in the seventeenth century, particularly in Holland, France, Italy and Spain. Reaching its zenith at a time when market economies, fuelled by trade and exploration, were expanding rapidly in scale and sophistication, still life painting not only depicted the fruits of wealth and the breadth of ownership, but was also a desirable commodity in itself. Often gathering together the products of the owner's estates with the exotic spoils of colonialism, ripe for the taking, the still life represented human control over the natural world, breaking the bonds of space and time. The four corners of the earth come together in this singular, domestic space: numerous species of flowers bloom simultaneously, every fruit is in season, diverse objects gain a pictorial equivalence and everything has its price.

However, there is tension inside the frame of some still life paintings, precisely when their domain extends beyond the local. The unity of the domestic zone is fractured by displays of wealth and commerce, the tactile qualities of humble objects and foodstuffs – rendered so precisely by the medium of oil paint – left behind when the objects become shiny or alien. Norman Bryson, in his

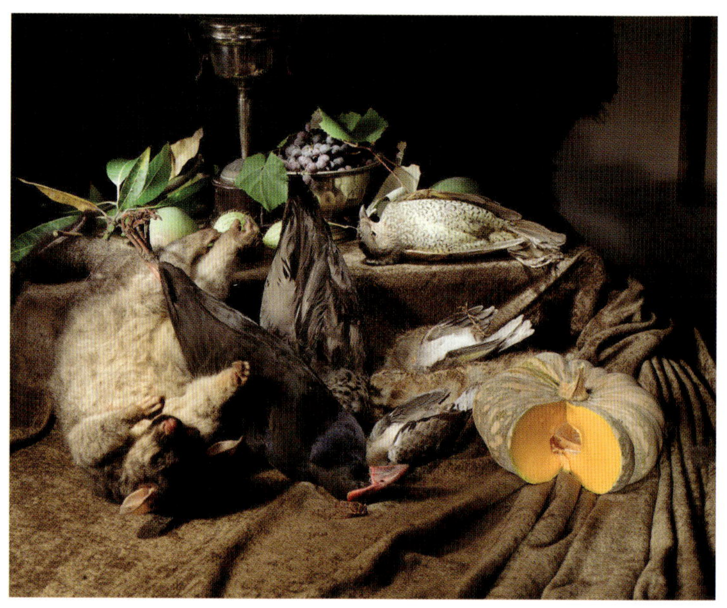

Possum with five birds (2003)

Tasmanian swamp hen with apples (2005)

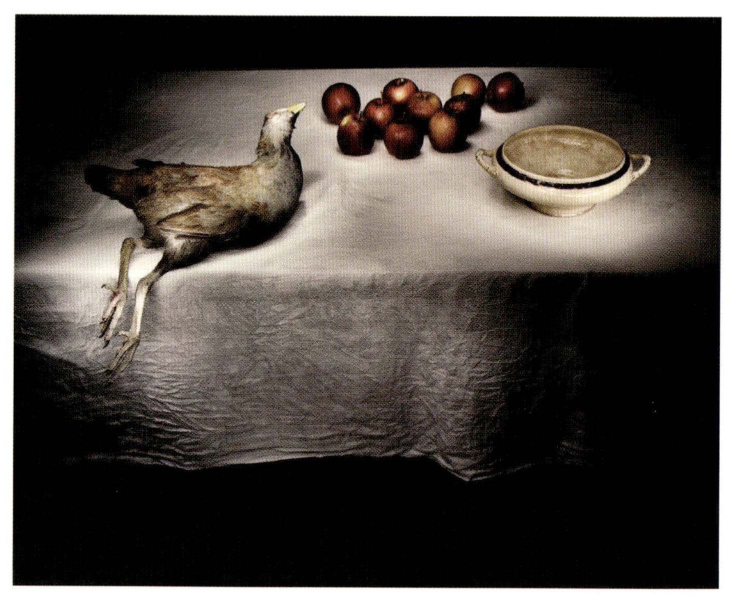

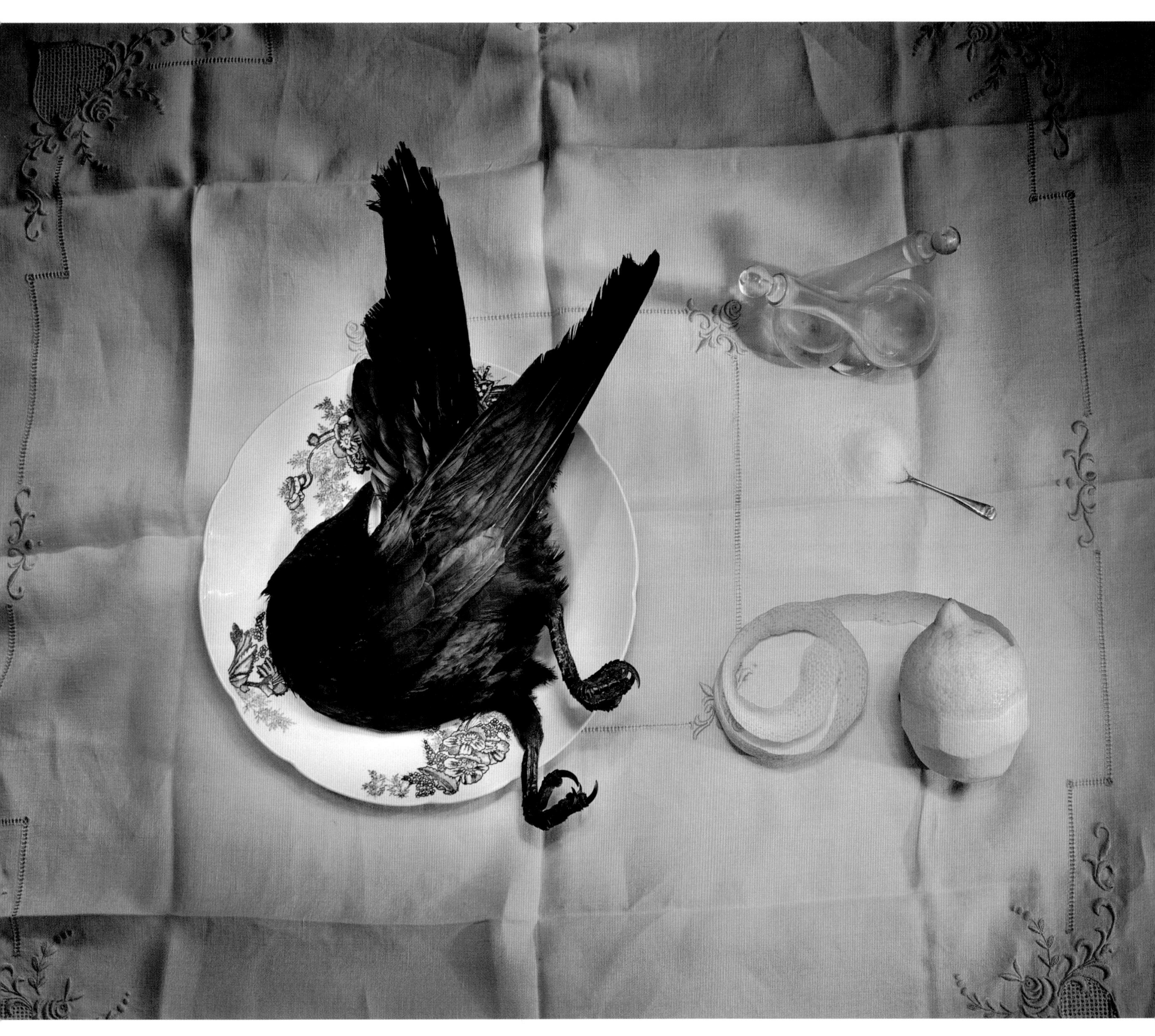

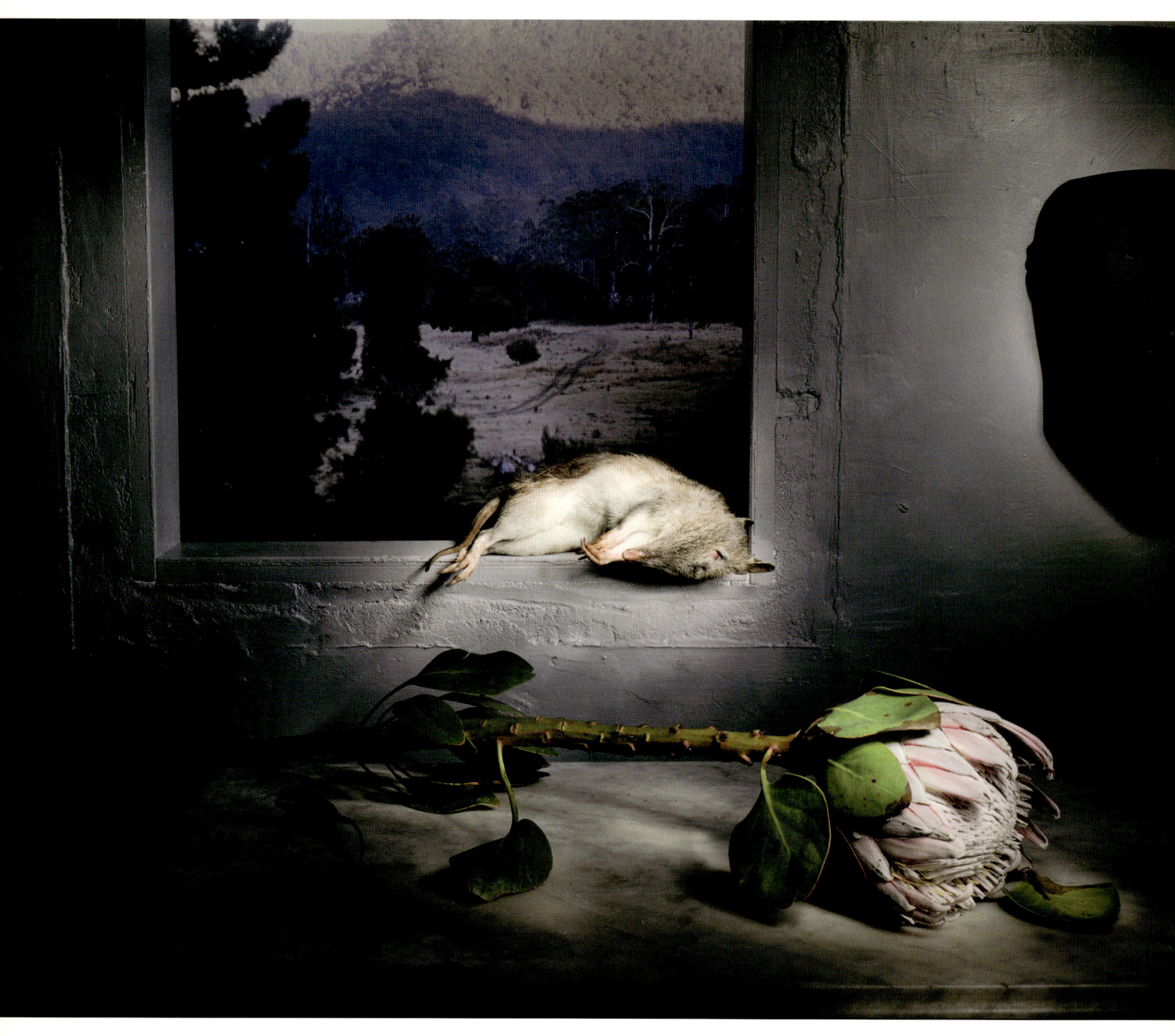

78   *Marsupial with Protea* (2004)

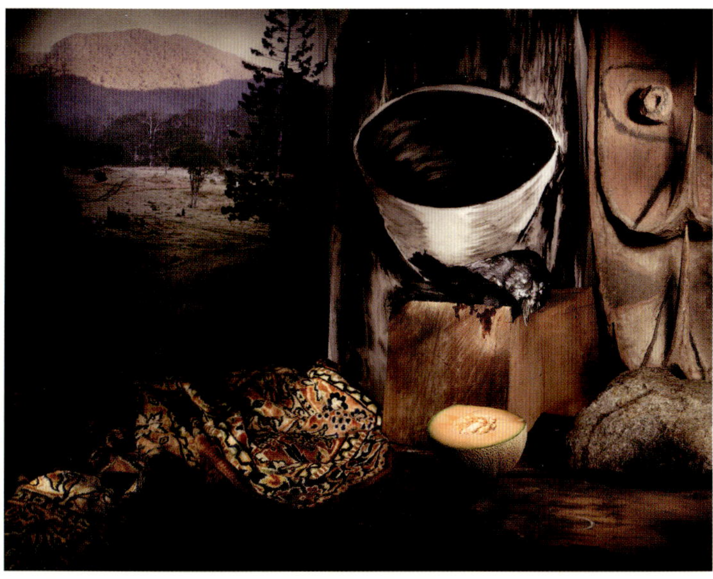

Raven, rock and rockmelon (2003)

Kitchen view and mask (2003)

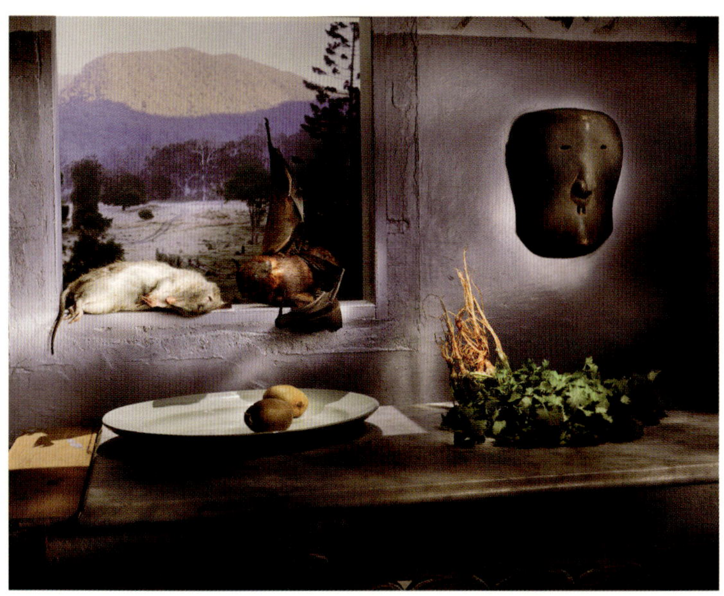

indispensable writing on still-life painting, notes that in these works, the table becomes like a graveyard, and the treasure house 'where objects come to die'.[1] The space of the still life in these paintings opens out to vast horizons, and the distances between people grows as competition and market forces overtake the communal coming together of the humble table.

It is this tense and unresolved, not to mention deathly, aspect of still life painting that is also present in Drew's works. The idea of the local is instantly made problematic: the animals are Australian natives, while the objects, fabrics, flowers and fruit are from Australia, Europe, Asia, Africa and the Pacific. In *Raven rock and rockmelon*, for example, a Persian carpet and a large mask from New Guinea are featured, while in *Kitchen view with mask*, kiwi fruit and coriander are arranged on a marble bench, overlooked by another large New Guinean mask. The corpses of a fruit bat and a long-nosed potoroo lie on the window sill, beyond which can be seen a vista of an Australian bush hill. *Marsupial with Protea* features a more tightly focused view of the same room and outlook, with the potoroo draped alone on the sill, and a dramatically lit African protea flower on the bench. The hermetic space of the still life opens onto a wide natural landscape, while the items of a cosmopolitan kitchen form stylish and knowing arrangements.

In the process of producing her still lifes, Drew creates a sequence of displacement's. The most obvious is the translation of historical painting into contemporary photography, a strategy utilised since the dawn of the photographic medium. Yet it is a relatively simple transformation, as evidenced by the popularity of photographic still life from the beginning. The 'mechanical' nature of still life painting, rendering intimate, inanimate objects realistically with an absence of narrative, makes it easy to simulate in a photograph. The directness of still life finds a parallel in the function of the camera in photography, often considered as a tool of replication rather than of creative endeavour (Drew herself has exploited the passivity of the camera in her work, stating that 'For me the camera is a stupid recorder, predictable, open'[2]). For these very reasons, both photography and still life painting have been considered in their time as relatively low forms of art, less worthy of esteem or scholarship than more ambitious genres such as narrative painting, a status that has been rectified substantially in recent decades.[3]

The second displacement is the location of the photographs in Australia. The context of European still life painting is that of a comfortable centre, the source of the genre and the natural site of its subject, with its connotations of wealth and privilege. Transferred to peripheral Australia, with its strange, awkward animals and rugged landscapes, the European fabrics and tableware appear here as ghostly and forlorn, pervaded by the melancholy that accompanies all colonial attempts at approximating the old country. In *Rosella in alabaster*, the brilliant colours of the bird appear jarring against the monochromatic fruit bowl and muted wood panelling behind, the brazen thrust of its body a contrast to the filigreed fruit bowl and overhanging picture frame. In *Plate and fruitbat*, the blue and white design of resting kangaroos on the china plate recalls the famed Willow pattern, itself an eighteenth-century British emulation of a Chinese design. The idealised, bucolic scene of Australian nature is slyly undercut by the lifeless body of the bat; its tightly curled wings having offered little protection against human threat.

The third key shift is in the replacement of fish, game or domesticated animals with wildlife. Drew's removal of 'use value' from the animals depicted provides much of the visceral shock of the images, as there is senselessness to their deaths. There is no further 'life' for these creatures as food; they will merely be discarded. In this sense, they represent an even greater severance of connection with nature, as they have no preordained human relationships. Still life painting is marked by its absence of human figures, yet every object within it bears the trace of human endeavour: farming, fishing, manufacture and trade, as well as eating, drinking and collecting. The animals in Drew's photographs correspond to none of these functions or processes. Their wildness is extreme, with no relation to the domestic environment in which they are placed. Their only attribute is death.

Because of this, the *Australiana* series relates most strongly to the *vanitas* subgenre of still life painting; allegorical pictures that contain various references to death and decay. Reminders of the transience of life and its worldly pleasures, *vanitas* paintings may include worm-infested fruit, wilting flowers, cracked china, skulls or timepieces amongst their arrangements. With their tone of Protestant moralism, *vanitas* paintings presented their owners with dire warnings against overindulgence and hubris, while contradictorily being luxury objects

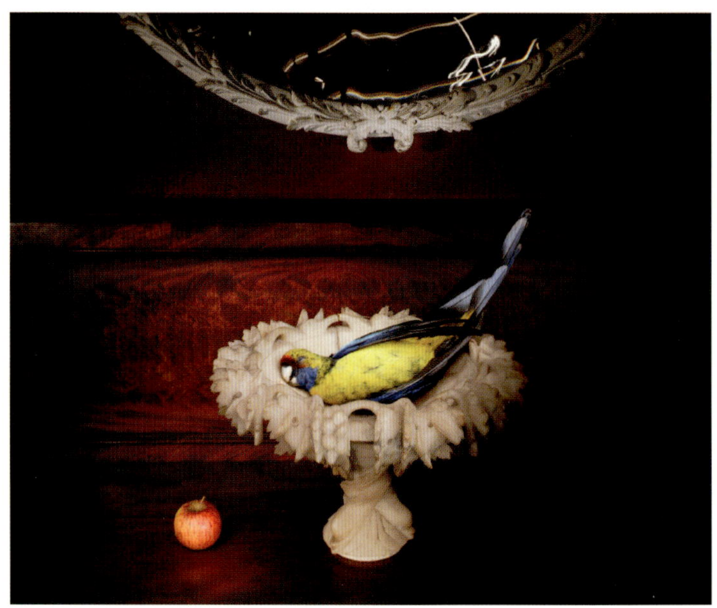

Rosella in alabaster (2006)

Fruitbat with plate (2003)

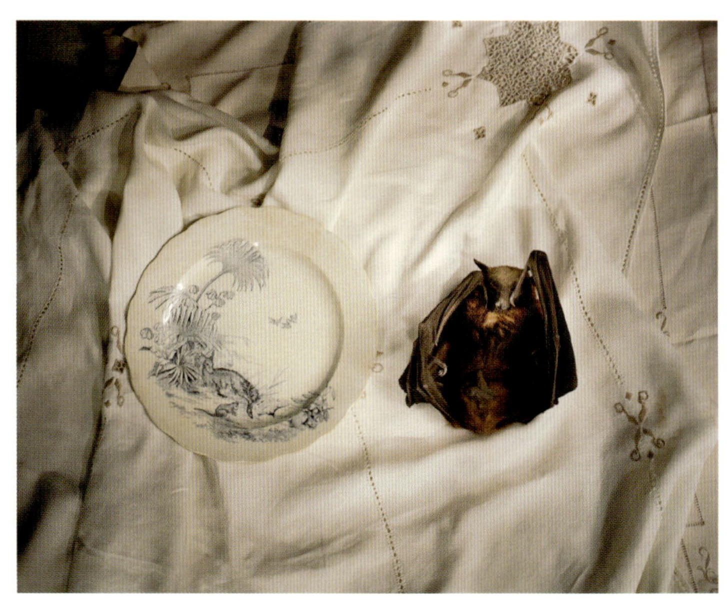

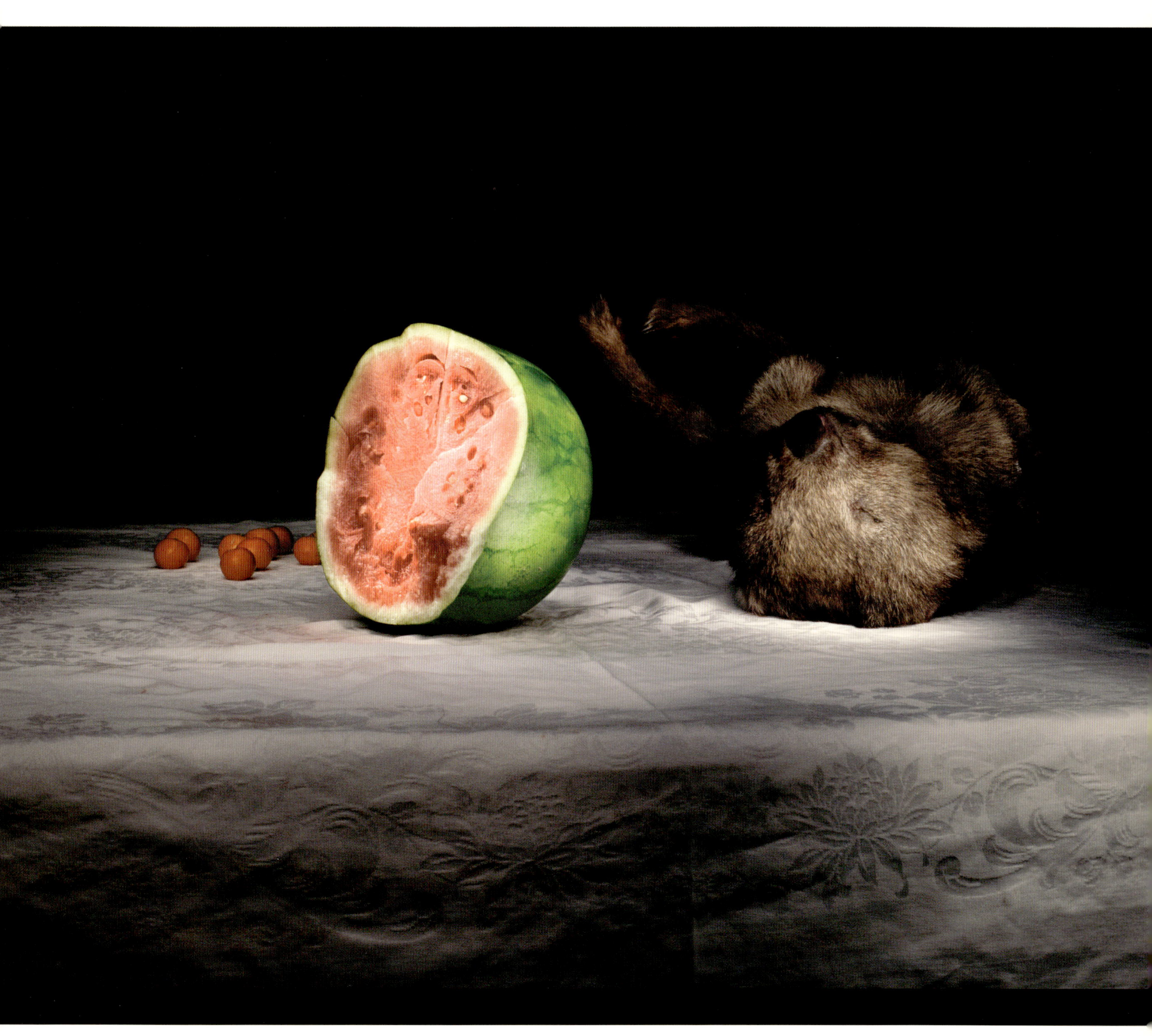

themselves.[4] Drew's work also embraces this paradox, using seductive, desirable photographs to make her point; yet the message is clear. Inside the homes of the well-informed, comfortable middle class, who recycle their rubbish and donate to good causes, lie the tools of destruction. Our lifestyles are deadly, and ultimately finite.

Russell Storer

[1] Norman Bryson, 'Abundance' in *Looking for the Overlooked: Four essays in Still Life Painting*, London: Reaktion Books, 1990, p.128.

[2] Marian Drew, interview by Alexandria McClintock, *Eyeline*, Autumn 1992, p.25.

[3] The explosion of critical writing about photography in the 1970's was followed by its increasing use by artists in the 1980's and its growing profile in the art market in the 1990's. Similarly, still-life painting has undergone critical reassessment in the second half of the twentieth century, by scholars such as Bryson, Charles Sterling, Sybille Ebert-Schifferer and William Gerdts, with a proliferation of books and exhibitions on the genre, both historical and contemporary.

[4] Bryson, pp.115-117.

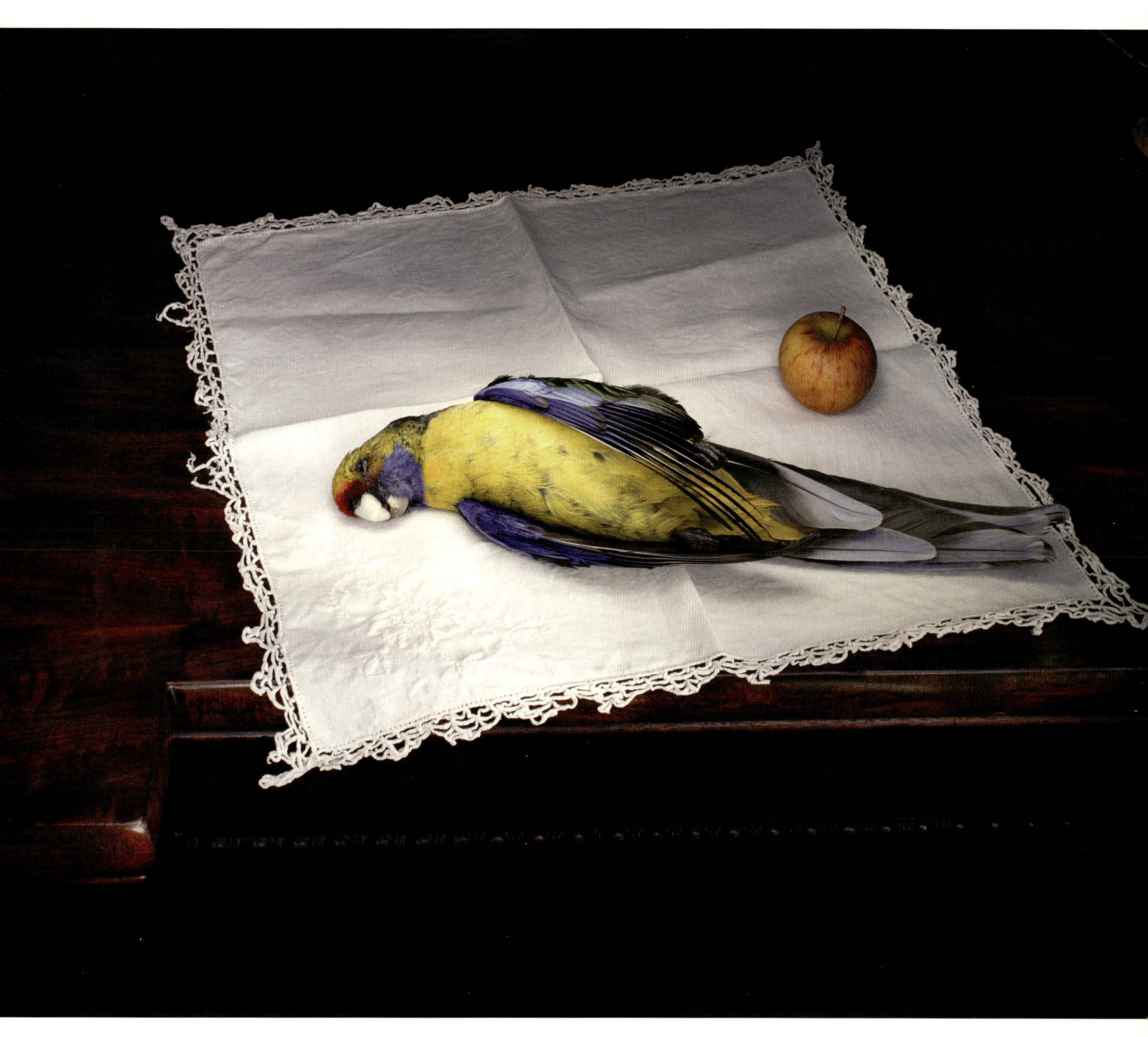

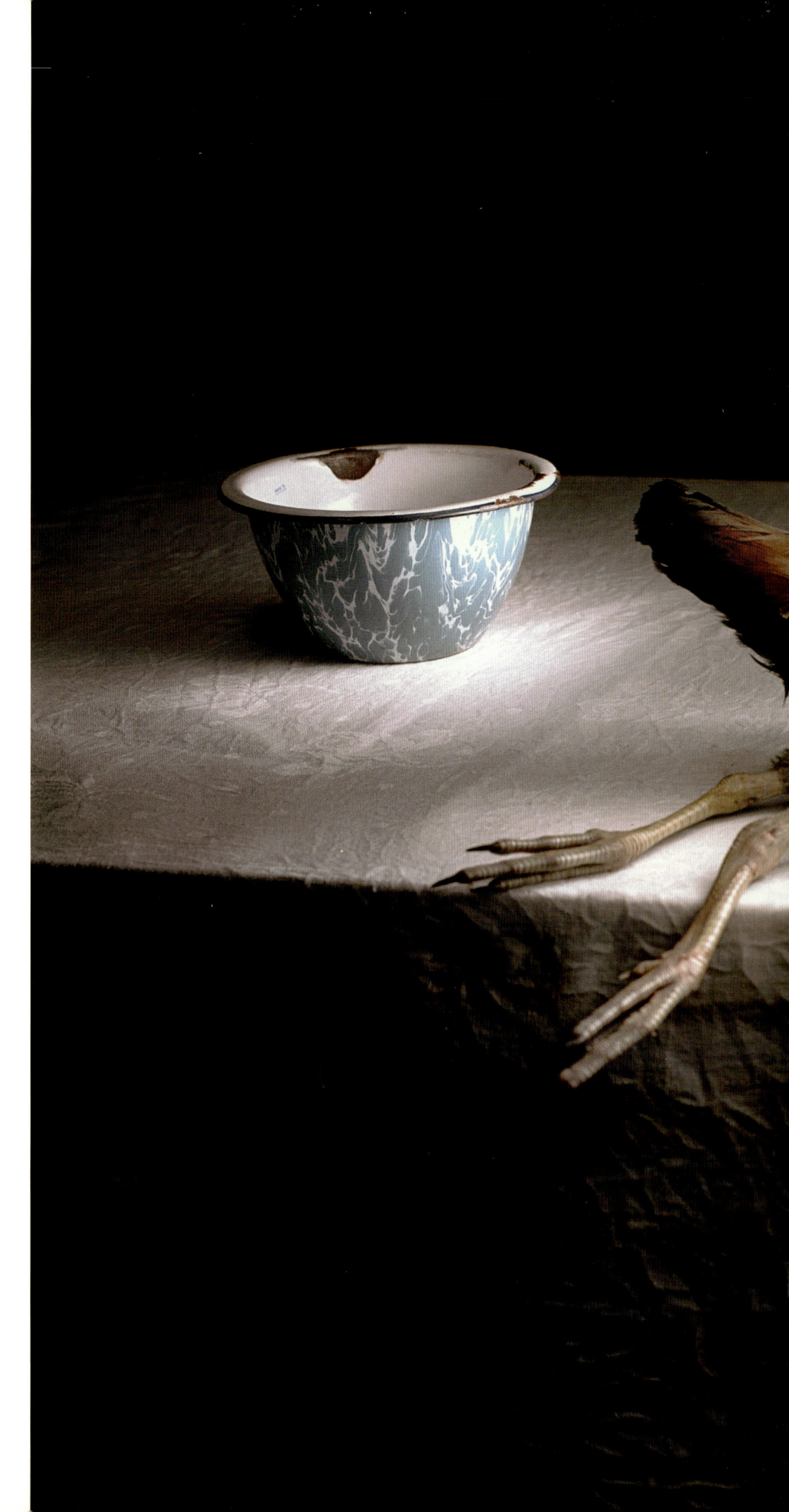

   Swamp hen with candle (2005)

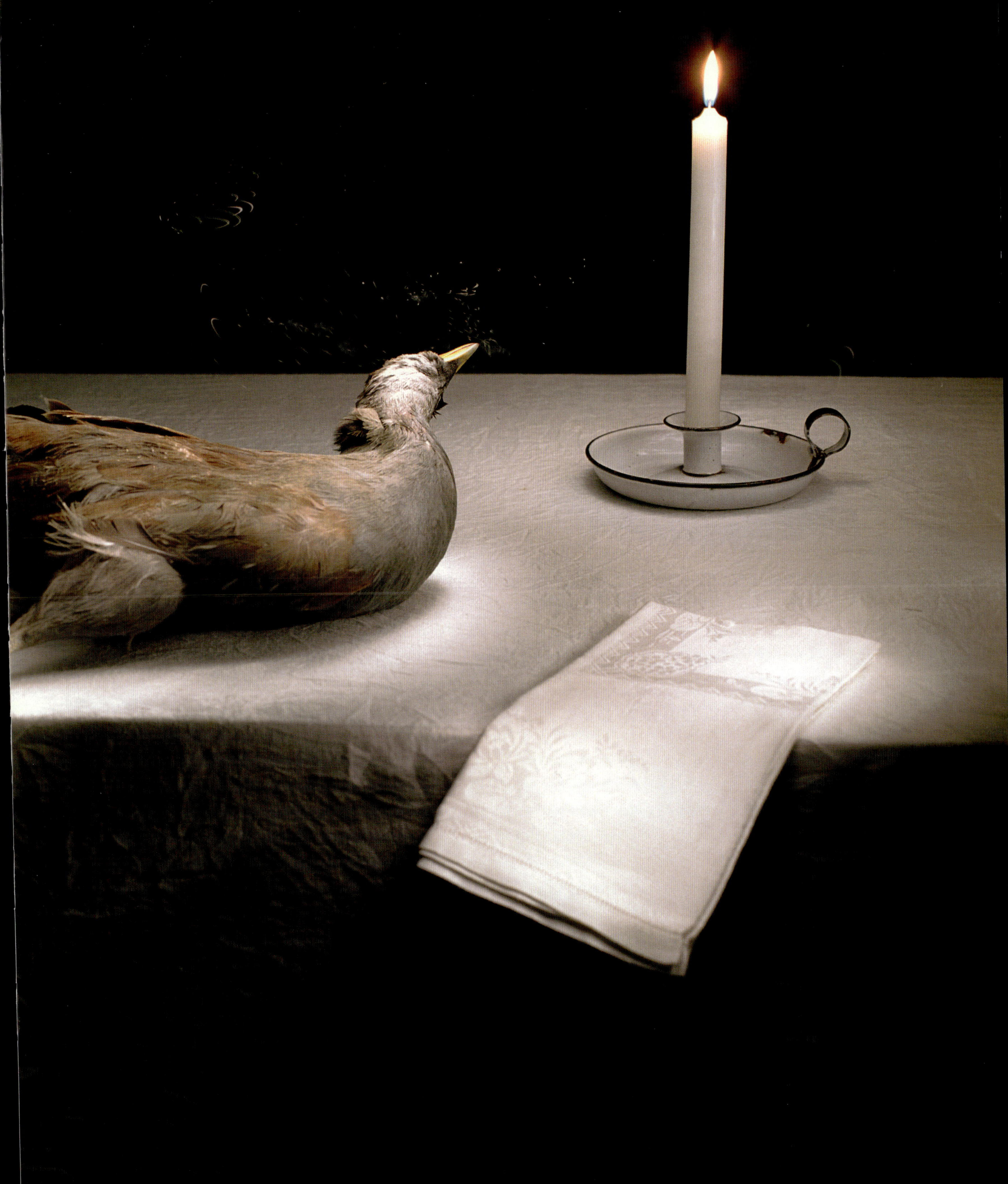

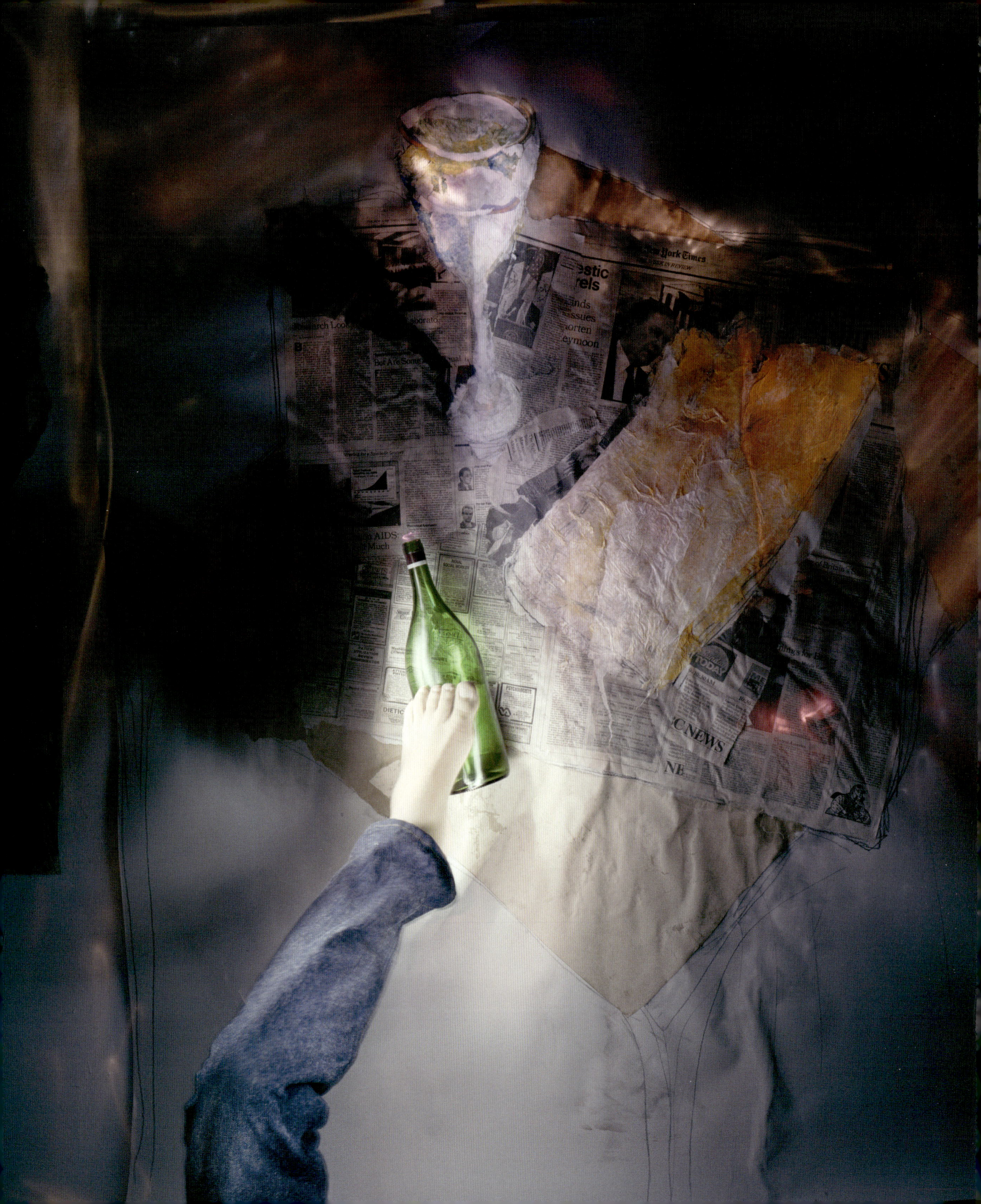

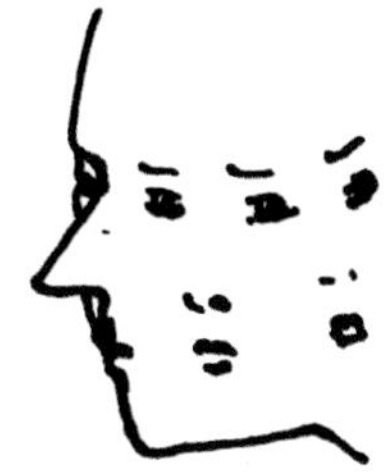

Projecting voices

I'm the sort of person that projects voices onto dogs, which is ok, except that recently my border collie seems to be developing a rather severe lisp. This personification although dangerous I admit, in its simplification and human centric perspective of animals, is for the same reasons a joyous activity. Projecting of one idea over another, I have continued since *Bush Projections* 1984, when I projected images of urban colours and environments onto ghost gum trees. Home, garden, and travel, has provided rich material for my art practice that shifts between drawing, installation, photography and video, setting up dialogues between media. Drawing a playful and thoughtful engagement between media and site, forms the basis of my art practice.

In photography I work with film, because chemical sensitivity to light and an open aperture gives me the long exposures I need to process light and action with subtlety and detail. Through a dialogue with drawing, sculpture and photography, motifs have developed in my work that revolve around water, animals, vessels, holes, dreams, death and the human form. These motifs emerge recurrently in my practice that draws on the site specific, rituals of the everyday, the repetitious and the domestic interactions between people, objects and things.

One enchanting aspect of photographic process for me is when the film is introduced to the developer. Developer is intended to reward this action with an image, but one can never be sure. There are several such acts of faith in the making of my photographic work. The act of painting with light is so variable with torch size, reflective or unreflective surfaces, distance, aperture, movement and speed, available light, battery charge, and my ability to remember, that there is always a significant gesture of faith when making an exposure. It is this act of adventure in the making of photographs and the mystical return of the image that forms a gratifying cycle in photographic production.

By making my marks in the space time of photography,

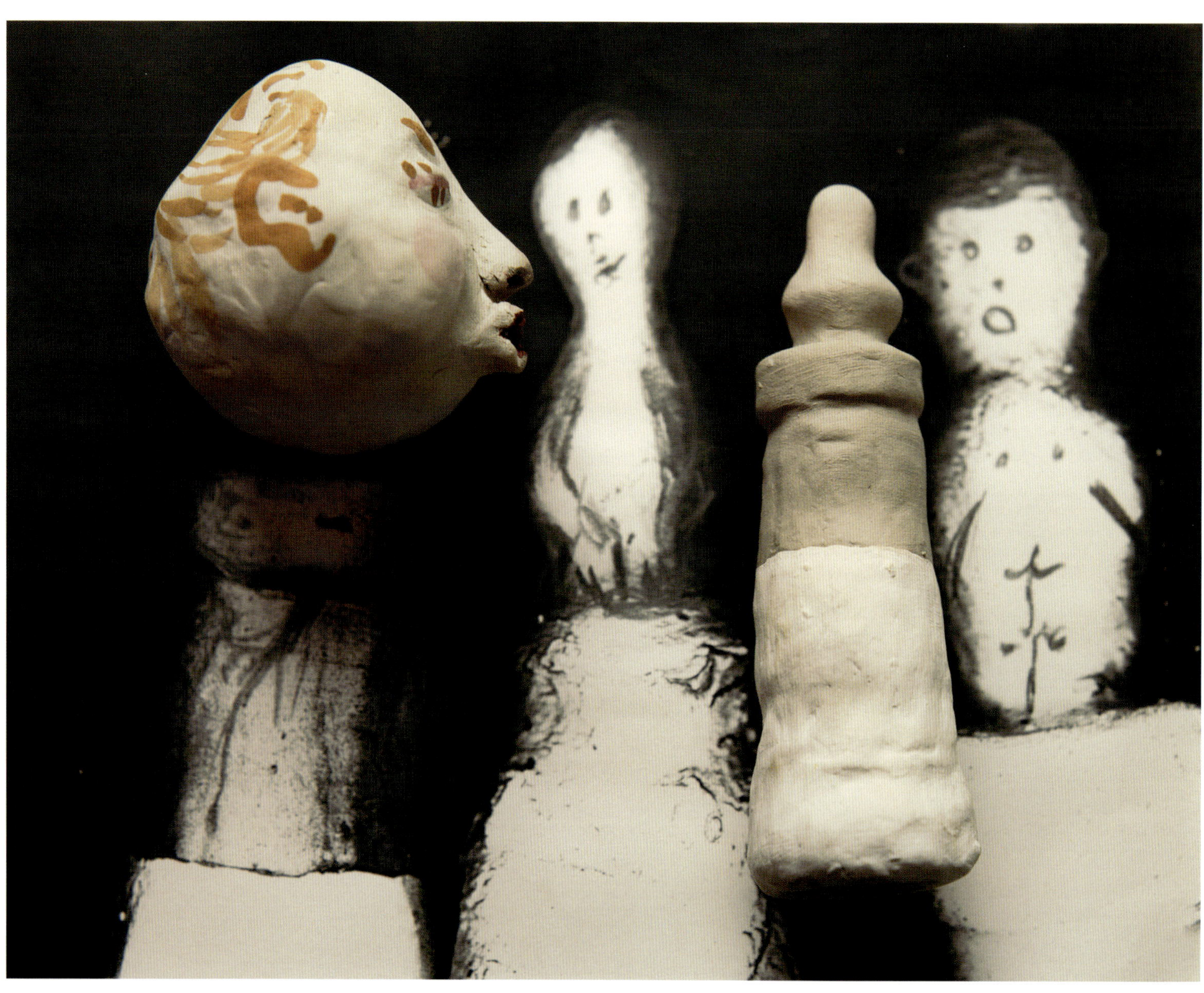

88   *Bottle with head* (1996)

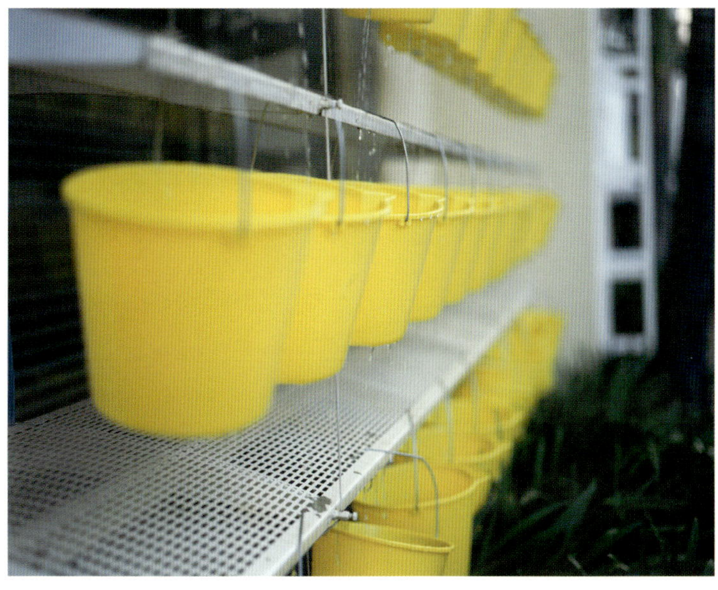

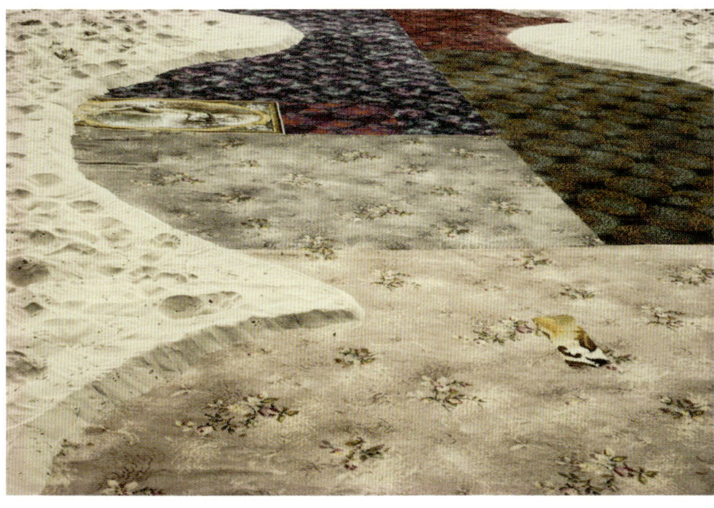

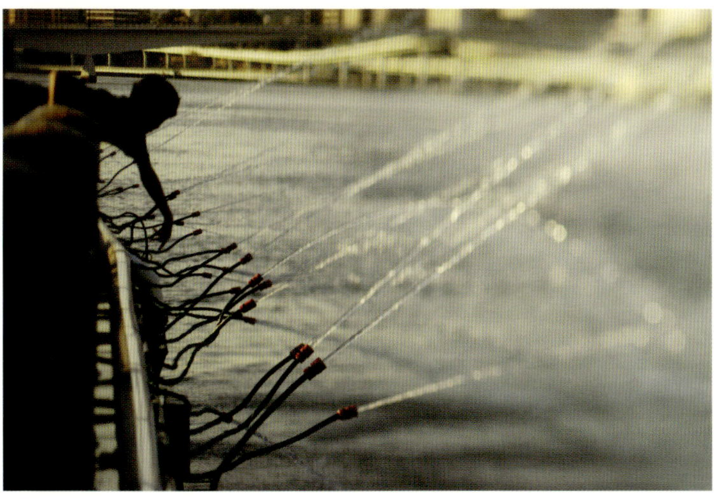

my gesture is implicit in the materiality of that which I photograph, the landscape and domestic environment in which I live. Photographic recording is capable of welding and solidifying hybrid forms, liberating ephemeral material from decay, time and distance. Walking a line, driving a mower, or throwing sand, through photography, can become activities through which to draw in time. Painting with light, or rather moving in front of the camera into the frame, applying light to the subject over time and through movement of the body, is an extension of the photographer's gesture which has become clearly integrated into the image.

I recognize in my practice the opportunist exploiting everyday experiences, collaborating with events, to create a pool of images through which I hope to discover and reflect, perspectives beyond the self. Processes to generate counterpoints and extend perspectives have included collaborations, the distortion of traditional techniques, hybridized materials and processes, and significantly, the encouragement of an attitude of playfulness in work that can have unplanned outcomes.

Several projects have involved collaborations with other artists, architects and designers, extending my exploration of materials and site. *Axeminster*, 'Sculpture By the Sea' Noosa (1998), an installation with Bruce Reynolds and Rex Roubin, consisted of forms inlaid into the sand , each made of joined patterns of Axeminster carpets, swept after the tide. *Bucket Up* (2001) Royal Australian Institute of Architects building, Brisbane, with Larry Weston, was an installation of red and yellow buckets, repeated units that formed a fountain of dripping buckets, in organized rows. *Scribble* (2004) another fountain installation was constructed with, Simon Laws. Using a large immersed pump to elevate river water at high pressure through domestic hoses, water was projected in a scribble action back into the river. Strobe flashes lit the water at night freezing the water visually mid air. *Awake /Asleep* a distant collaboration with German artist, Thomas Bachler, has been a postal project that employs chance to unite northern and southern hemispheres on negatives. Acting as tourists in our own country the image of one site and event pivots within the other.

top to bottom: *Bucket up* (2001), *Axeminster* (1998), *Scribble* (2004)

The photographic process is important and beautiful to me because of the stable and elegant support it lends to ideas. If photography holds a mirror to our ideas and our place in the world, then an inquiry into the mode of representation provides a map through which we may understand the representation.   Decoding the representation we metaphorically if not physically find our position within it. This is why I prefer my constructions to be made physically in the world and documented on film rather than arranged on a computer.

By developing tools that embrace childish curiosity, chance, absurdity, dislocation and location, I hope to disturb dominant perspectives. By misusing or hybridizing materials in an attitude of play, I hope to promote images that question traditional representations of our being in the world. Raising two children encourages the perspective of 'other', and has aided in diffusing the borders between domestic activity and art, as has sharing studios with my artist partner Bruce Reynolds.

However it is the dislocation of travel that has provided some of the most powerful opportunities to shift perspective and has been influential in defining my art practice over time. Through awareness of location one ultimately discovers the here and now as a site and as a mirror for the body and ideas.

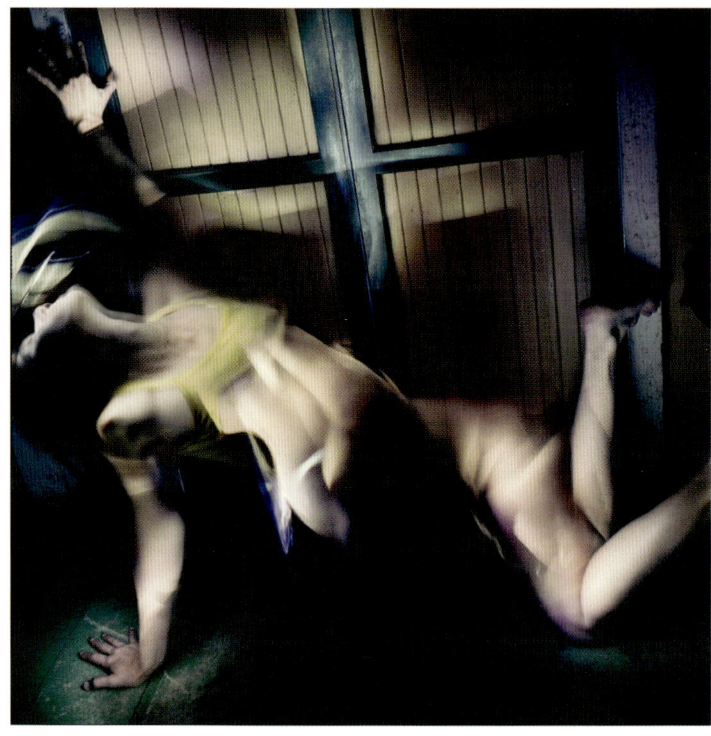

Figure with cross (1988)

Untitled (1990)

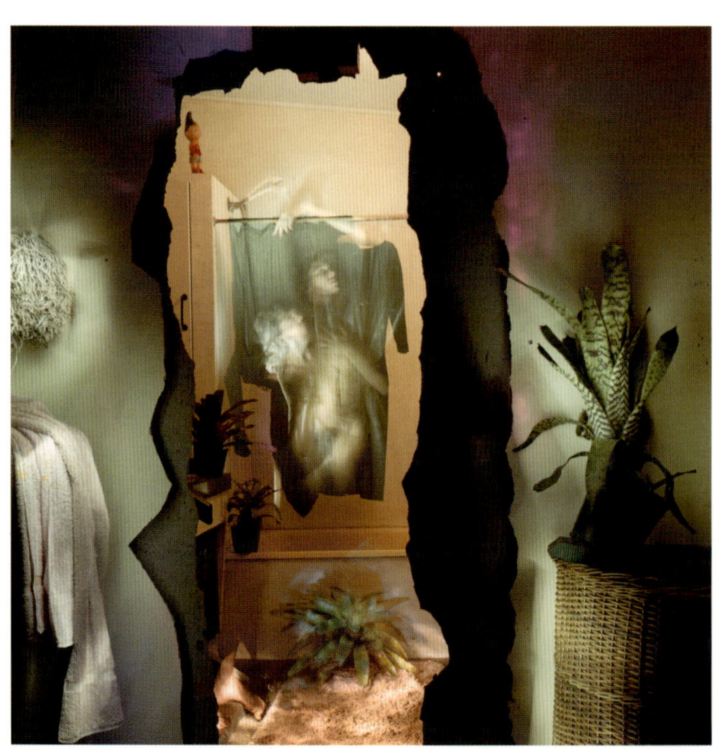

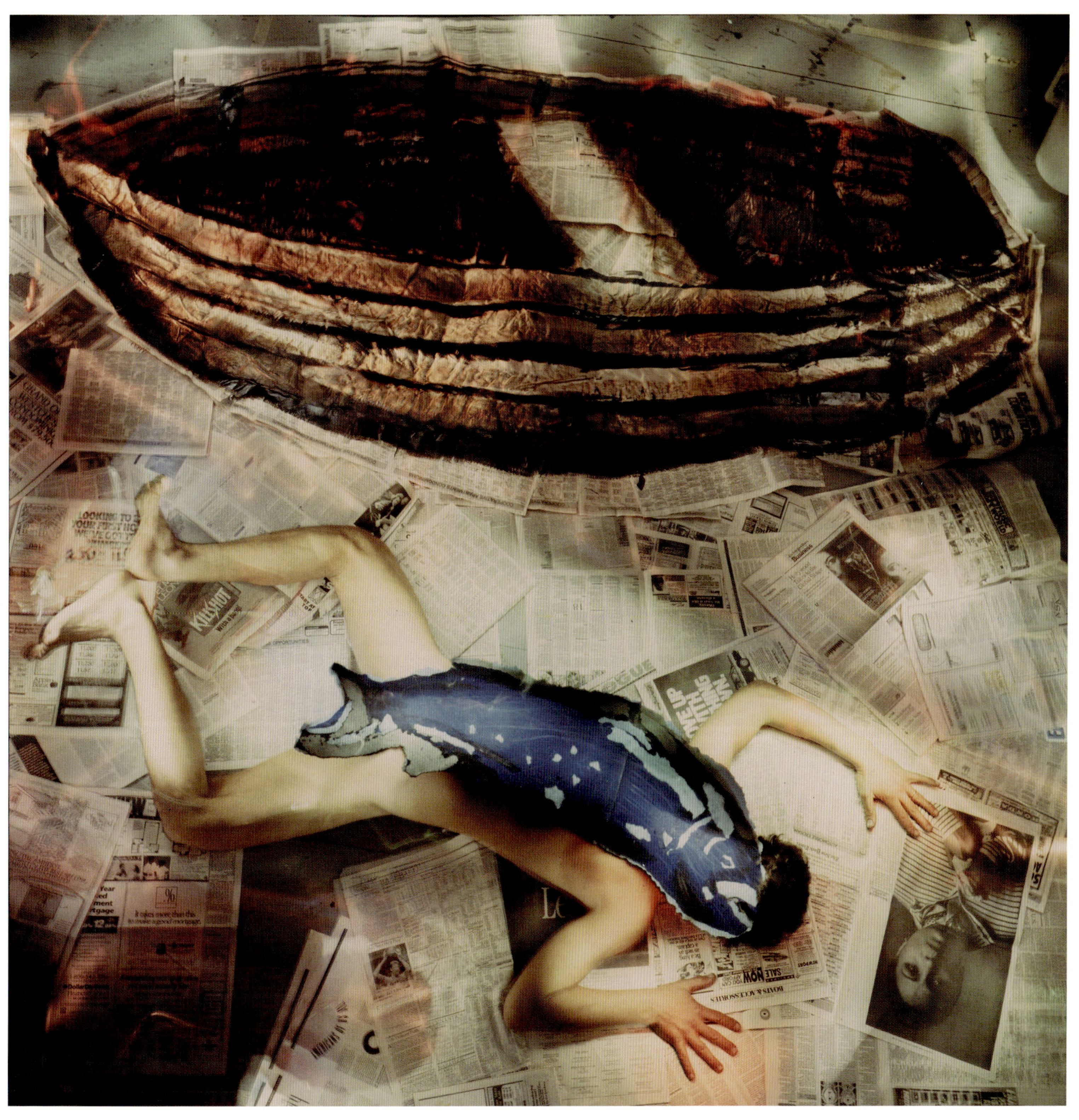

Fishman (1990)

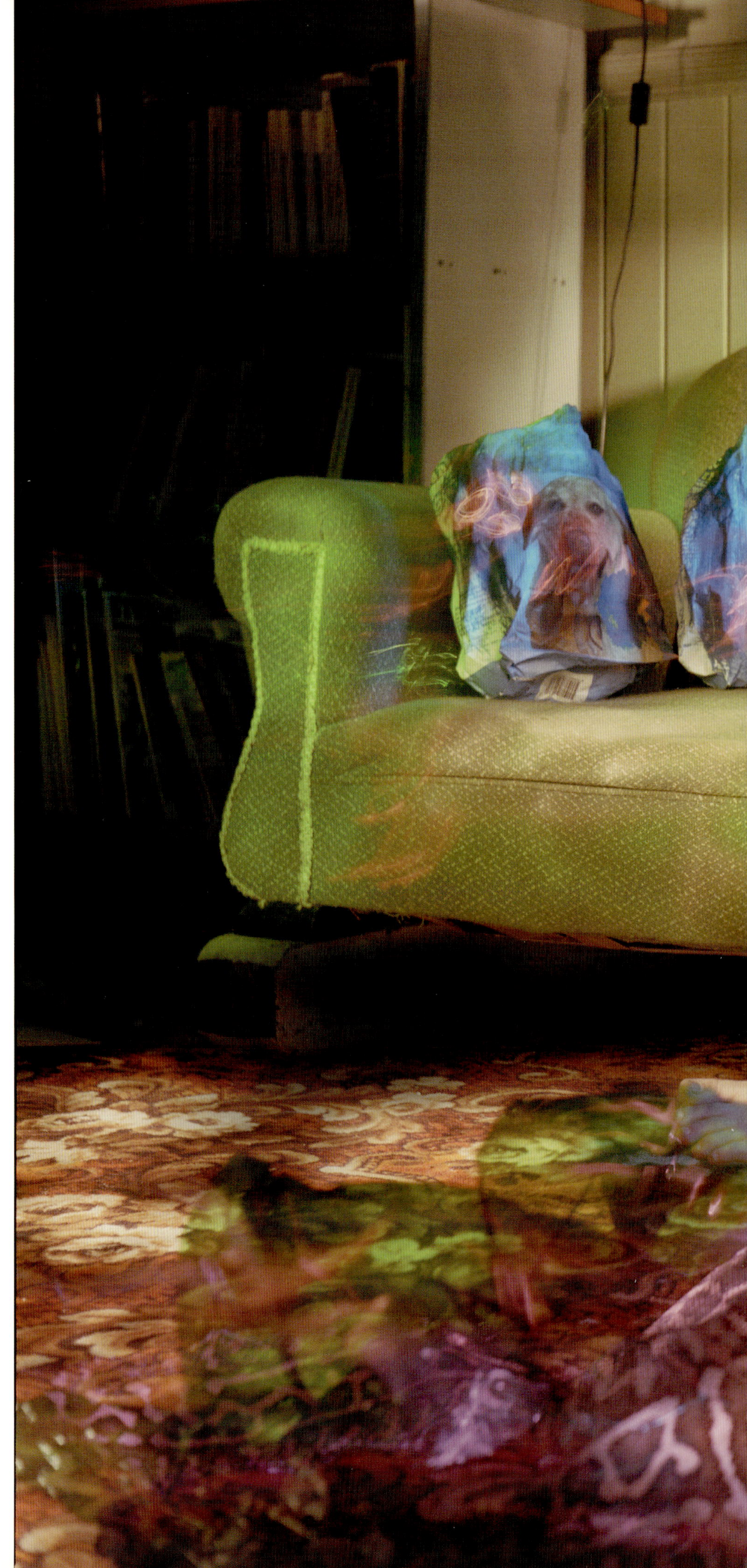

    Figure with three dogs (1988)

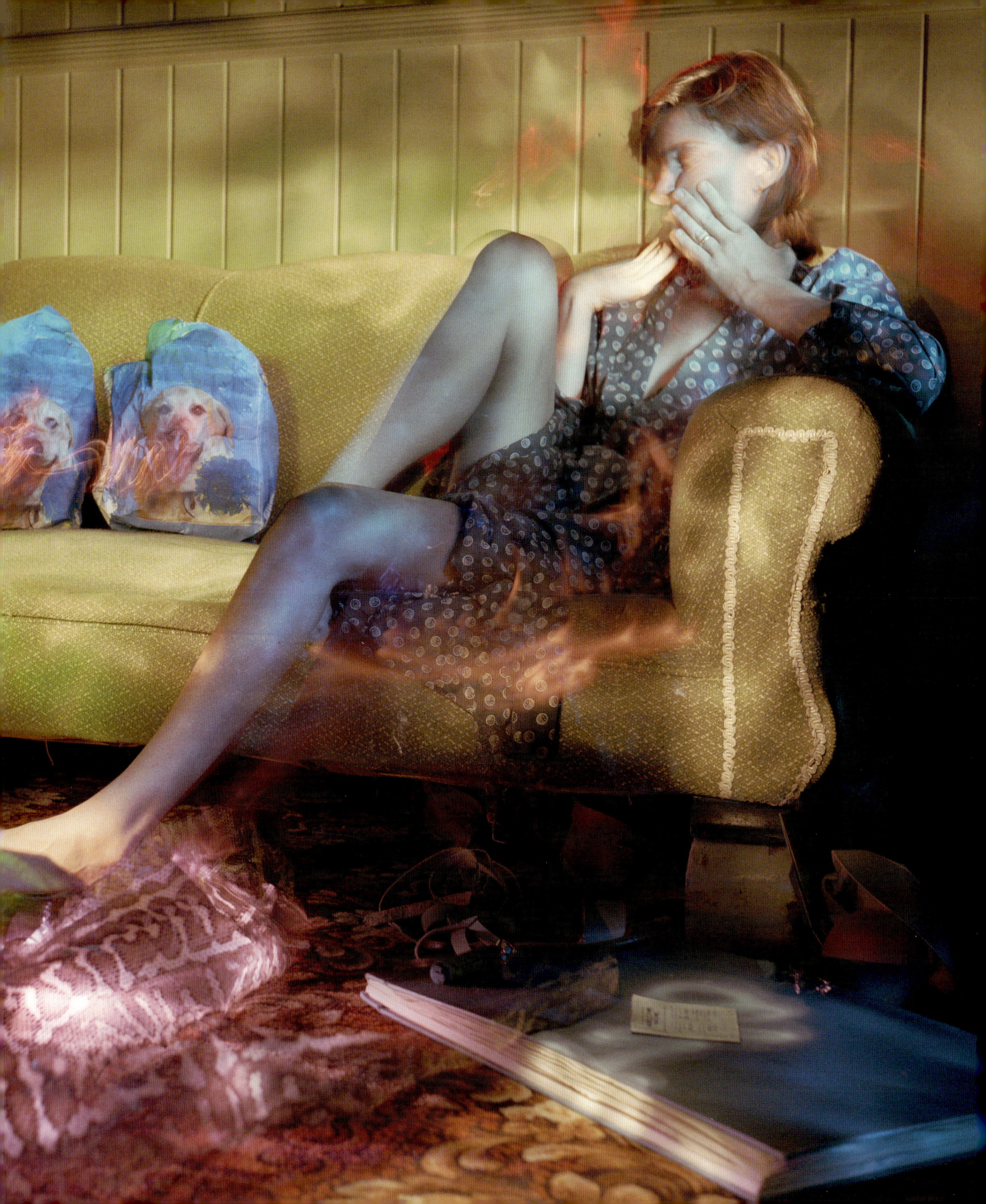

Marian Drew

Born Bundaberg, Australia 1960. Lives and works in Brisbane, Australia.

Selected education

1980-84	Bachelor of Visual Art, Letter of Merit, Canberra School of Art.
1984-85	Post graduate studies, Kassel University, (HBK) Germany.
1984-85	DAAD Scholarship, German Government Academic Exchange. Travelled and studied art in Europe with Dyason Bequest NSW Art Gallery.

Selected solo exhibitions

2006	Robin Gibson Gallery, *Still Life*, Sydney, Australia.
2005	Dianne Tanzer Gallery, *Still Lives*, Melbourne, Australia.
2005	Queensland College of Art, *After the Fall* (Video and sound Installation), Brisbane River Festival, Australia.
2005	Queensland Centre for Photography, *Still Lives*, Brisbane, Australia.
2004	Robin Gibson Gallery, *Australiana*, Sydney.
2003	Gallery 482, *Australiana*, Brisbane, Australia.
2000	Powerhouse, *Marian Drew: Powerhouse Photographs*, Brisbane, Australia.
1999	Gallery 482, *This is what I think*, Brisbane, Australia.
1998	Gallery 482, *Black and White*, Brisbane, Australia.
1997	Bundaberg City Art Gallery, *Marian Drew: A Retrospective* (1984-1997), Bundaberg, Australia.
1996	Brisbane City Art Gallery, *Persistent Blindness*, Brisbane, Australia.
1994	Australian Centre for Contemporary Art, *Things Past*, Melbourne, Australia.
1993	Sommerville House, *Artist in residence exhibition*, Brisbane, Australia.
1990	Ray Hughes Gallery, *New York Series*, Sydney, Australia.
1988	Photospace Gallery, *Marian Drew*, CSA, Canberra, Australia.
1987	Ray Hughes Gallery, *Marian Drew*, Brisbane, Australia.
1986	Gallery Etoile, FNAC (Fonds National D'Art Contemporain), *Bush Projection Series*, Paris, France.
1985	Kassell University Gallery, *Drinnen-Draussen*, Kassel, Germany.
1983	Images Gallery, *Marian Drew*, Sydney, Australia.

Selected group exhibitions

2006	QUT Art Museum, *Animal as Allegory*, Brisbane, Australia.
2005	Brisbane City Hall, *ARC Biennale*, Brisbane, Australia.
2005	QCA Gallery, *Chance Encounters*, Brisbane, Australia.
2004	Redland Art Gallery, *Sleight*, Redland, Australia.
2004	Kassel Kunstverein, *Back to Kassel, part 3, Photography*, Kassel, Germany.
2004	Queensland Centre for Photography, *Camera Less - Another Viewpoint*, Brisbane, Australia.
2002	Australia Centre, *Awake/Asleep: Thomas Bachler/Marian Drew*, Berlin, Germany.
2001	European Kunst Akademie Trier, *Styx: Projektionen Video Art*, Trier, Germany.
2001	Gallery 482, *Buried in Cotton*, Brisbane, Australia.
1999	Queensland College of Art Gallery, *Spatial Eclipse/Temporal Anchorings*, Brisbane, Australia.
1998	Australian Centre for Photography, *Signature works: 25 Years of Australian Photography*, Sydney, Australia.
1996	Canberra School of Art Gallery, *A Matter of Making*, Canberra, Australia.
1996	Queensland Art Gallery, *The Power to Move*, Brisbane, Australia.
1994	Queensland Art Gallery, *Mad and Bad Women*, Brisbane, Australia.

Self-portrait (1984)

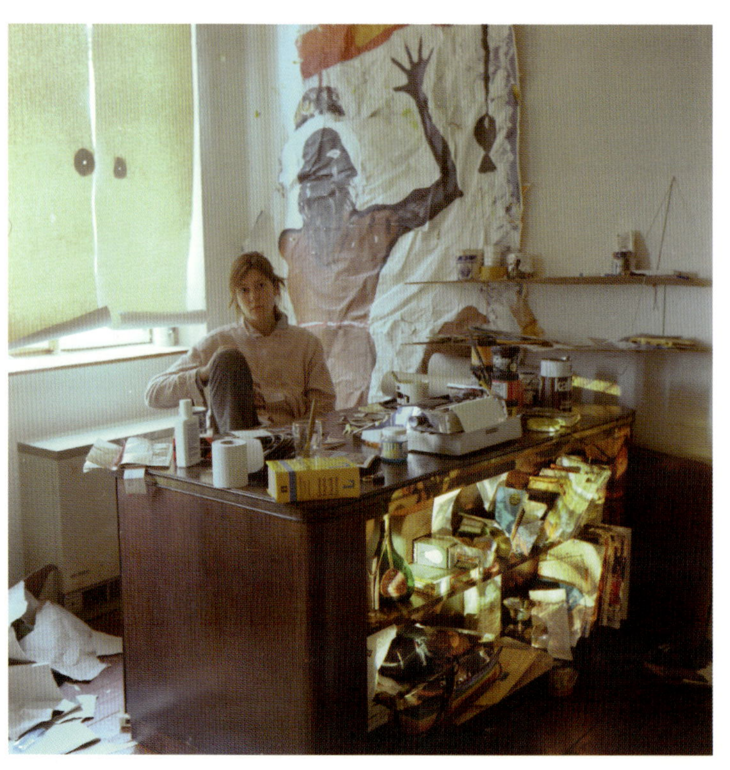

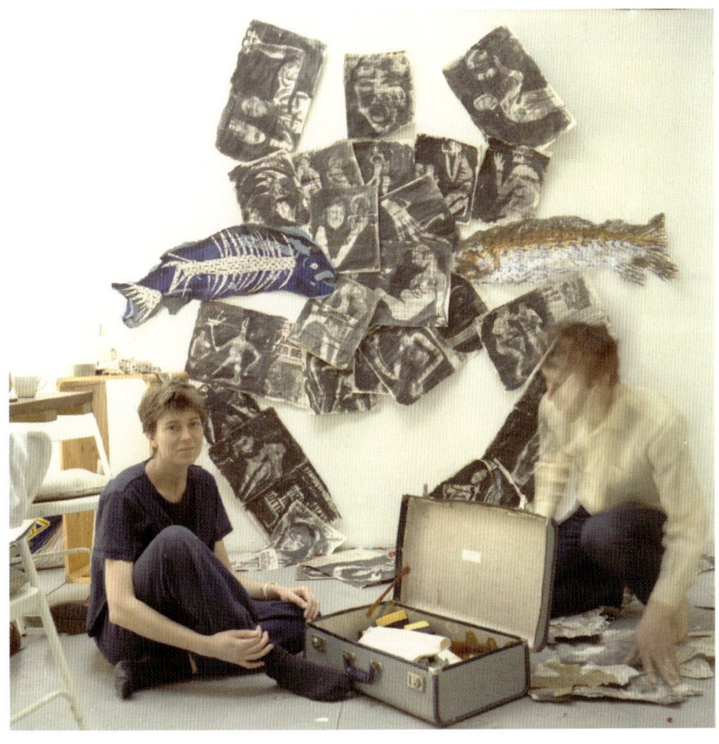

Self-portrait (1989)

Self-portrait (2006)

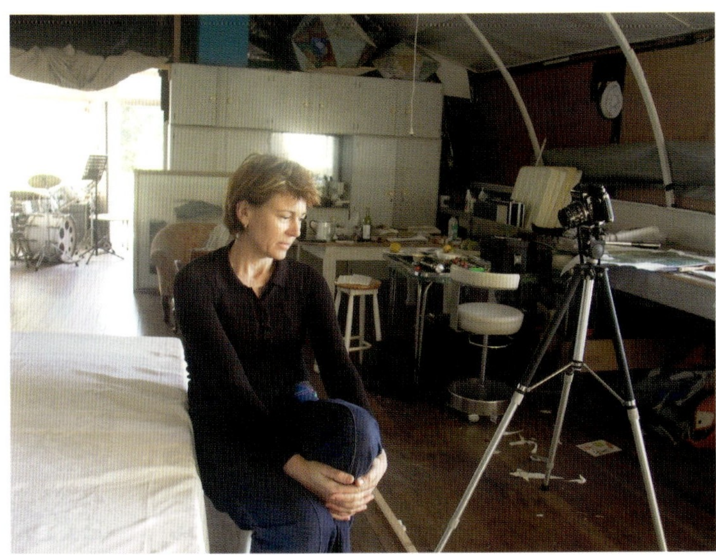

1993	Queensland Art Gallery, *First Asia-Pacific Triennial of Contemporary Art*, Brisbane, Australia.
1992	Institute of Modern Art, *Twentieth Century Fops*, Brisbane, Australia.
1992	Camerawork, *Empty Land*, London and travelling the United Kingdom.
1990	Art Gallery of South Australia, *Fragmentation and Fabrication*, Adelaide, Australia.

1989	Queensland Art Gallery, *Private Views - Public Spaces*, Brisbane, Australia.
1987	Queensland Art Gallery, *Moments in Queensland Contemporary Art*, Brisbane, Australia.
1986	Institute of Modern Art, *Young Contemporaries*, Brisbane, Australia.
1985	Neue Galerie, *Kasseler Kunstler*, Kassel, Germany.
	Australian Centre for Contemporary Photography,
1983	*New Light*, Sydney, Australia.
1982	Australian Craft Council Gallery, *Three Canberra Artists*, Canberra, Australia.

Selected public commissions:

2005-2006	Environmental Protection Agency National, Parks and Wildlife, *Seven Great Walks*, exhibition and publication.
2004	River Festival, *Scribble*, water sculpture collaboration with Bulind designer, Simon Laws, Brisbane, Australia.
2003-2004	Brisbane Magistrate Court, 5 floors continuous photograph, unique photogram, Brisbane, Australia.
2003	Queensland Academy of Sport, 18 meter glass wall, Brisbane, Australia.
1998	Brisbane City Council, photographic artwork for the Powerhouse Performing Arts Complex, Brisbane, Australia.

Selected collaborative projects:

2001-2006	*Awake/Asleep*, photographic project with Thomas Bachler, Australia/Germany.
2004	*Scribble*, installation with Simon Laws, Brisbane, Australia.
2001	*Bucket up*, installation with Larry Weston, Brisbane, Australia.
1998	*Axeminster*, installation with Bruce Reynolds and Rex Roubin, Noosa, Australia.

Selected collections:

National Gallery of Australia, Canberra, Australia.
Brisbane City Council, Brisbane, Australia.
Queensland University of Technology, Brisbane, Australia.
Art Gallery of South Australia, Adelaide, Australia.
Queensland Art Gallery, Brisbane, Australia.
The Daryl Hewson Collection, Brisbane, Australia.
University of South East Queensland, Toowoomba, Australia.
Griffith University Collection, Brisbane, Australia.
Waverley City Council Art Collection, Melbourne, Australia.
Fonds National D'Art Contemporain (FNAC), Paris, France.
Artbank, Sydney, Australia.

list of works

p.2:
Pink Strawberry Honey (1992)
Sommerville House Artist Recidency
Type C print, 90x120cm

p.4:
Untitled (2000)
Powerhouse series
Type C print, 100x125cm

p.7:
Light sticks Lake McKenzie (2006)
National Parks series
Archival pigments on cotton paper, 70x90cm

p.9:
Boat Lake McKenzie (2006)
National Parks series
Archival pigments on cotton paper, 70x90cm

p.10:
Fraser Cross (2006)
National Parks series
Archival pigments on cotton paper, 70x90cm

p.12:
Sequoia (1995)
National Park of California
Archival pigments on cotton paper, 70x90cm

p.13:
Chinese Landscape Gold Coast (2006)
National Parks series
Archival pigments on cotton paper, 70x90cm

p.14:
Inlet Mackay Highlands (2006)
National Parks series
Archival pigments on cotton paper, 70x90cm

p.15, top:
Tree + circle Whitsunday (2006)
National Parks series
Archival pigments on cotton paper, 70x90cm

p.15, bottom:
Untitled (2000)
Powerhouse series
Type C print, 100x125cm

p.16, top:
Monolith (2000)
Powerhouse series
Type C print, 100x125cm

p.16, bottom:
Cross and figure (2000)
Powerhouse series
Type C print, 100x125cm

p.17:
Blue rectangle (2000)
Powerhouse series
Type C print, 100x125cm

p.18:
Satin and lino (1992)
Wynnum History series
Type C print, 90x120cm

p.19, top:
Skinning (1992)
Wynnum History series
Type C print, 90x120cm

p.19, bottom:
Bogman (1992)
Wynnum History series
Type C print, 90x120cm

p.20:
Bandicoot with Quince (2005)
Australiana/Still Life series
Archival pigments on cotton paper, 85x110cm

p.21, top:
Galah in landscape (2003)
Australiana/Still Life series
Archival pigments on cotton paper, 75x90cm

p.21, bottom:
Magpie with Pawpaw (2005)
Australiana/Still Life series
Archival pigments on cotton paper, 85x110cm

p.22, top:
Hole 1 (1982)
Holes series
Silver gelatin print, 35x35cm

p.22, bottom:
Hole 3 (1982)
Holes series
Silver gelatin print, 35x35cm

p.23:
Untitled (1982)
Holes series
Silver gelatin print, 35x40cm

p.25:
NY Aquarium (1997)
Darkroom series
Silver gelatin print, 80x110cm

p.27:
Studio landscape (1997)
Darkroom series
Silver gelatin print, 60x85cm

p.28:
One of four ways to fly (1) (1985)
Germany series
Type C print, 40x40cm

p.30, top left:
Untitled (1983)
Bush Projections series
Type C print, 40x40cm

p.30, top right:
Untitled (1983)
Bush Projections series
Type C print, 40x40cm

p.30, bottom left:
Untitled (1983)
Bush Projections series
Type C print, 40x40cm

p.30, bottom right:
Untitled (1983)
Bush Projections series
Type C print, 40x40cm

p.31:
Untitled (1983)
Bush Projections series
Type C print, 40x40cm

p.32, top:
The Dance 1 (The Argument) (1988)
Wynnum series
Type C print, 45x45cm

p.32, bottom:
The Dance 2 (1988)
Wynnum series
Type C print, 45x45cm

p.33:
Cabbage and bowl (1988)
Wynnum series
Type C print, 45x45cm

p.34:
Late Fall (1990)
New York series
Type C print, 90x120cm

p.35:
Animal interference (1990)
New York series
Type C print, 90x120cm

p.36-37:
Boats with swimmer (1990)
New York series
Type C print, 90x120cm

p.38:
**A beautiful and enduring myth
(with blue light)** (1993)
Wynnum History series
Type C print, 90x120cm

p.39:
A beautiful and enduring myth (1993)
Wynnum History series
Type C print, 90x120cm

p.40:
Paper and rock (1993)
Wynnum History series
Type C print, 90x120cm

p.41:
**Crude and cumbersome objects
frozen into place** (1993)
Sommerville House Artist Residency
Type C print, 90x120cm

p.42, top:
Clay and milk (1996)
Persistent Blindness exhibition
Type C print, 40x50cm

p.42, bottom:
Tree and milk (1996)
Persistent Blindness exhibition
Type C print, 40x50cm

p.43:
Still life with clay trees (1996)
Persistent Blindness exhibition
Type C print, 40x50cm

p.44:
Bottle and pear (1996)
Persistent Blindness series
Type C print, 100x130cm (detail)

p.45:
Untitled (1996)
Persisnt Blindness exhibition
Type C print, 40x50cm

p.46-47:
Yellow Cow (1996)
Persistent Blindness exhibition
Type C print, 100x130cm

p.48:
night day (2005)
Awake Asleep series, col. Thomas Bachler
Archival pigments on cotton paper, 70x90cm

p.50:
swimmer plaza (2002)
Awake Asleep series, col. Thomas Bachler
Archival pigments on cotton paper, 70x90cm

p.52-53:
photographer photographer (2005)
Awake Asleep series, col. Thomas Bachler
Archival pigments on cotton paper,
60x160cm

p.55:
horse castle (2002)
Awake Asleep series, col. Thomas Bachler
Archival pigments on cotton paper
70x90cm

p.56:
backyard schloss (2004)
Awake Asleep series, col. Thomas Bachler
Archival pigments on cotton paper
70x90cm

p.57:
landscape painting (2004)
Awake Asleep series, col. Thomas Bachler
Archival pigments on cotton paper
70x90cm

p.59:
garden sculpture (2004)
Awake Asleep series, col. Thomas Bachler
Archival pigments on cotton paper
70x90cm

p.60-61:
beach monument (2005)
Awake Asleep series, col. Thomas Bachler
Archival pigments on cotton paper,
60x160cm (detail)

p.63:
Shadow Matter (1999)
Light Matter series
Type C print, 70x90cm

p.64:
Three light forms (1999)
Light Matter series
Type C print, 70x90cm

p.65:
Three graces (1999)
Light Matter series
Type C print, 70x90cm

p.66-67:
Untitled (2004-2006)
Watergram series
Archival pigments on cotton paper,
90x150cm (detail)

p.68-69:
Wait a whiles (2004-2006)
Watergram series
Archival pigments on cotton paper,
90x150cm (detail)

p.70:
Tree of life (2001)
Pond series
Palladium print
70x90cm

p.71:
Untitled (2001)
Pond series
Palladium print
70x90cm

p.72-73:
After heavy rain (2001)
Pond series
Palladium print
70x110cm

p.74:
Pelican with turnips (2004)
Australiana/Still Life series
Archival pigments on cotton paper,
85x110cm

p.76, top:
Possum with five birds (2003)
Australiana/Still Life series
Archival pigments on cotton paper,
85x110cm

p.76, bottom:
Tasmanian swamp hen with apples (2005)
Australiana/Still Life series
Archival pigments on cotton paper,
85x110cm

p.77:
Crow with salt (2003)
Australiana/Still Life series
Archival pigments on cotton paper,
85x110cm

p.78:
Marsupial with Protea (2004)
Australiana/Still Life series
Archival pigments on cotton paper,
85x110cm

p.79, top:
Raven, rock and rockmelon (2003)
Australiana/Still Life series
Archival pigments on cotton paper
75x90cm

p.79, bottom:
Kitchen view with mask (2003)
Australiana/Still Life series
Archival pigments on cotton paper
75x90cm

p.80, top:
Rosella in alabaster (2006)
Australiana/Still Life series
Archival pigments on cotton paper,
85x110cm

p.80, bottom:
Fruitbat with plate (2003)
Australiana/Still Life series
Archival pigments on cotton paper,
85x110cm

p.81:
Wambat with watermelon (2005)
Australiana/Still Life series
Archival pigments on cotton paper,
85x110cm

p.83:
Tasmanian Rosella with apple (2005)
Australiana/Still Life series
Archival pigments on cotton paper,
85x110cm

p.84-85:
Swamp hen with candle (2005)
Australiana/Still Life series
Archival pigments on cotton paper,
85x110cm

p.86:
Still life with bottle (1990)
New York series
Type C print
50x60cm

p.88:
Bottle with head (1996)
Persisten Blindness exhibition
Type C print, 60x70cm

p.89, top:
Bucket up (2001)
installation with Larry Weston
144 buckets, hoses and water

p.89, middle:
Axeminster (1998)
installation with Bruce Reynolds and
Rex Roubin, sand and carpet, 18x5m

p.89, bottom:
Scribble (2004)
installation with Simon Laws, pump, garden
hoses and river water, 36x6x6m

p.90, top:
Figure with cross (1988)
Wynnum series
Type C print, 50x50cm

p.90, bottom:
Untitled (1990)
Bathroom wall series
Type C print, 50x50cm

p.91:
Fishman (1990)
New York series
Type C print, 50x50cm

p.92-93:
Figure with three dogs (1988)
Wynnum series
Type C print, 50x50cm

p.94:
Self-portrait (1984)
Artist Residence, Germany

p.95, top:
Self-portrait (1989)
Artist Residence, New York

p.95, bottom:
Self-portrait (2006)
Artist studio, Hemmant

p.99:
Bed (1993)
Wynnum History series
Type C print
90x120cm

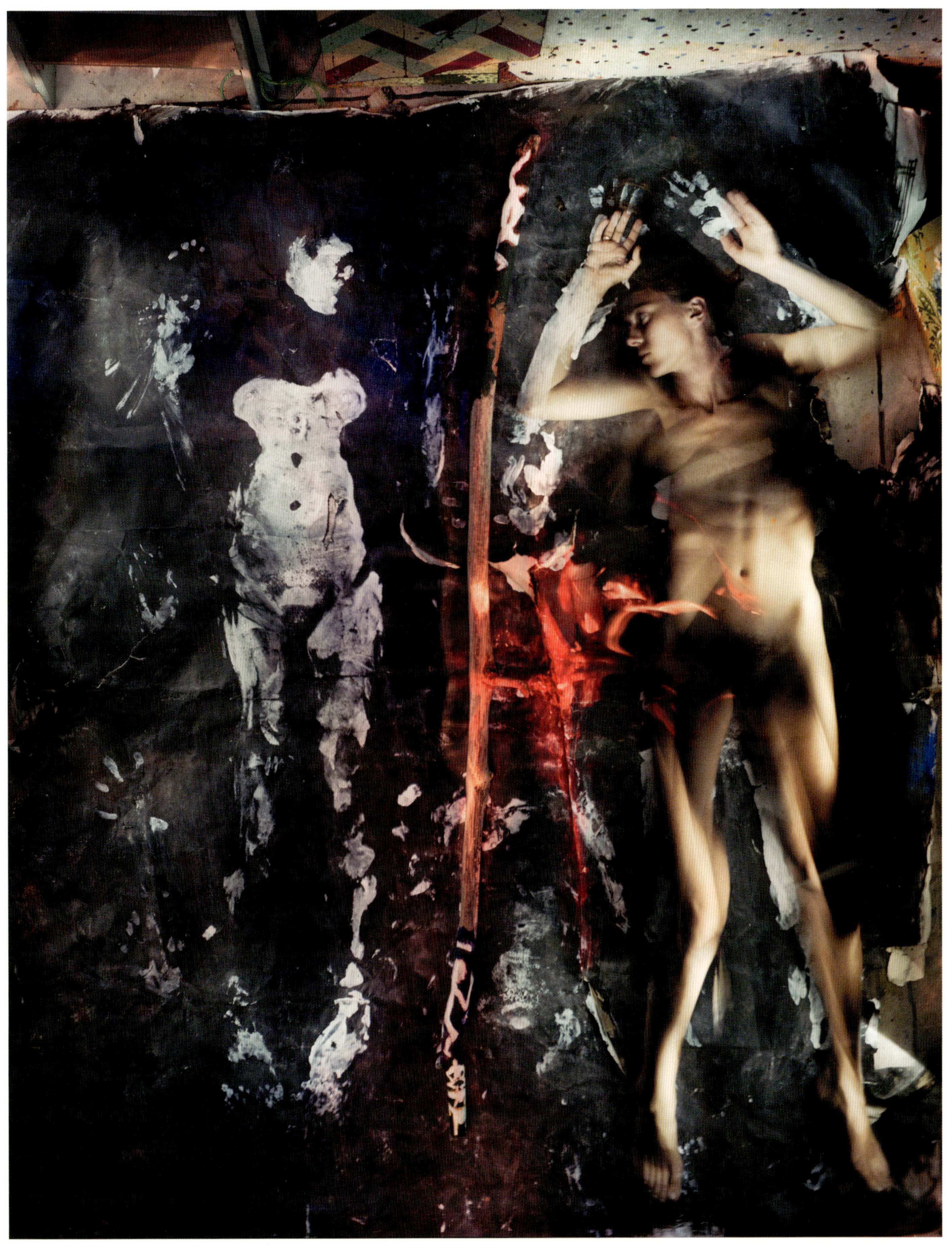

Bed (1993)

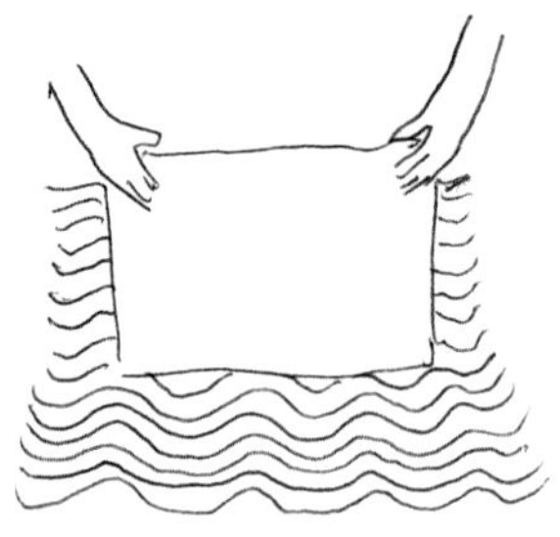

For my dad

I would like to acknowledge and thank the writers for their careful and intelligent texts, Alex Chomizc for his vision in filming the documentaries prior to this project, Bruce Reynolds, Thomas Bachler and Simon Laws for collaborations in art practice and Camilla Birkeland and Maurice Ortega for their professionalism, optimism and ability, in making this publication a reality. I would also like to thank Alex Scott, for the design and production of the DVD, Kris Carlon for the video interview, Martin Barry from Brisbane Digital Images, and thanks to family and friends for their continuing encouragement.

First published in 2006, Queensland Centre for Photography (QCP), on the occasion of the *Marian Drew: photographs + video works* exhibition at the Queensland Centre for Photography, Brisbane, Australia, 16 September - 15 October, 2006.

Exhibition curated by Maurice Ortega, Director, QCP

Queensland Centre for Photography
33 Oxford Street
Bulimba Qld 4171
Australia

www.qcp.org.au

Marian Drew is represented by
Dianne Tanzer Gallery, Melbourne; Robin Gibson Gallery, Sydney; QCP, Brisbane.

Designed by Camilla Birkeland, QCP.
Printed by 3E Innovative, Brisbane, Australia.
Printed on Sovereign Silk 180gsm.

© the Queensland Centre for Photography 2006
© text, Geoffrey Batchen, Dr Caroline Jordan, Anne Kirker, Dr Brigitta Olubas, Russell Storer, and Marian Drew 2006
© *Scribble* image, Sonja de Sterke 2004
© *Awake Asleep* images, Marian Drew and Thomas Bachler 2006
© all other images, Marian Drew 2006
All drawings have been taken from the artist's diaries.

This project was supported by the Queensland Government,
through an Art Queensland Major grant.

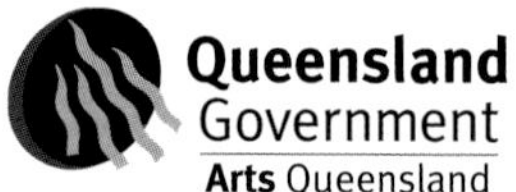

ISBN 0-9757720-1-5

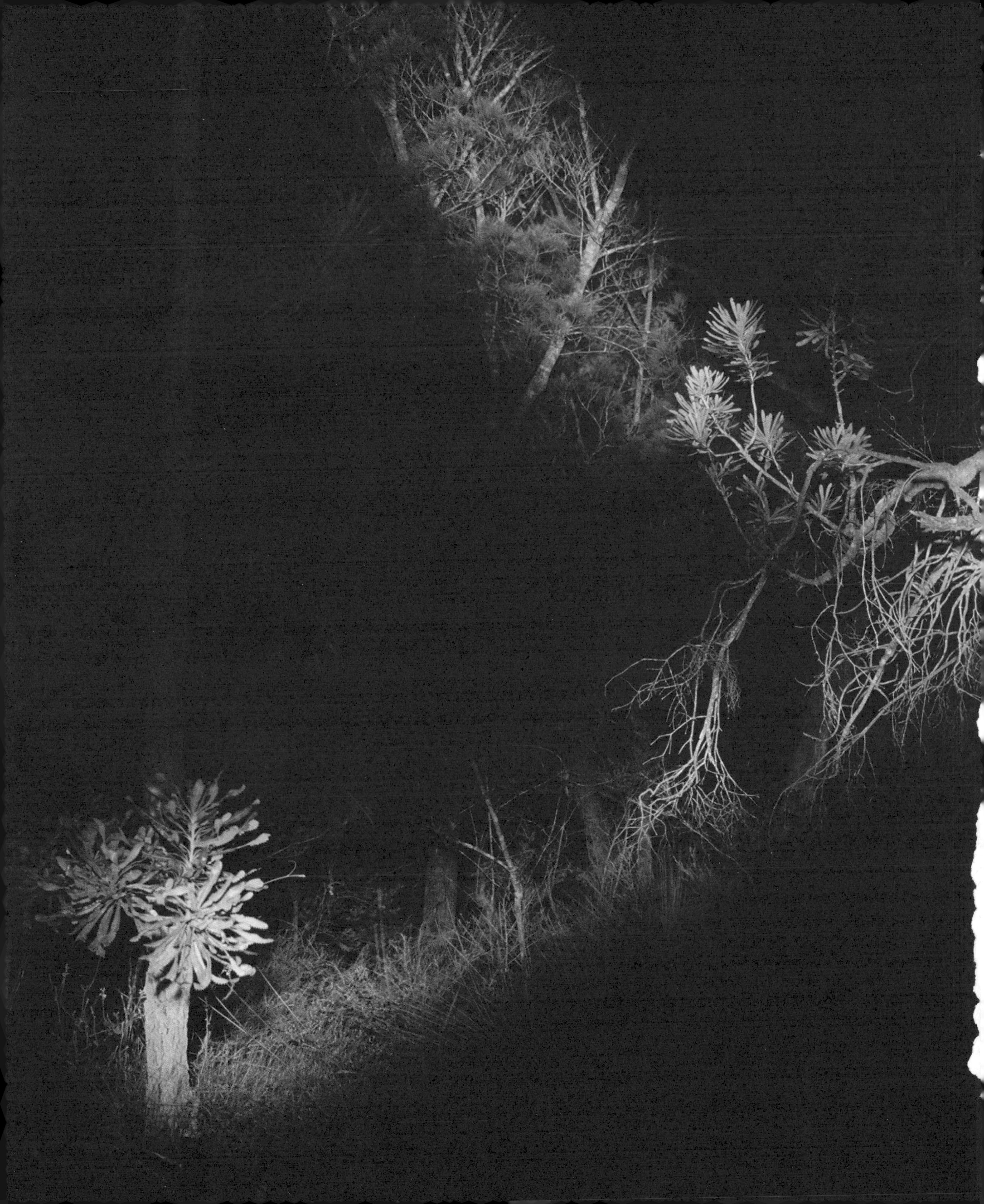